The Truth About You:

A Collection of Studies Revealing your Identity,

Position and Redemption IN Christ

(Second Edition)

Table of Contents

SECTION ONE

THE TRUTH ABOUT YOUR IDENTITY

(UNDERSTANDING YOUR INDETITY)

SECTION TWO

THE TRUTH ABOUT YOUR POSITION

(DEVELOPING THE WAYS OF ROYALTY)

SECTION THREE

THE TRUTH ABOUT YOUR REDEMPTION

(UNDERSTANDING HOW AND WHY YOU BECAME WHAT YOU ARE)

-Acknowledgments-

To my loving, wonderful wife Dr. Feleshia Borskey Young, Psy.D, you have done much to impact my life and propel me forward. Much of what others enjoy as I minister is the fruit of your constant love and prayers.

To my loving, wonderful daughter Kelsei Lubom, you are the motivation for my drive and the level of excellence in which I attempt to operate in.

To my parents Dr. Johnny and Emma Young, thank you for believing in me and leading me in the path of righteousness.

To Heavenly H.O.P.E Ministries, all of HBI and especially to my J. Young, International staff . . . Thank you for all you do to make me better as a husband, father, son and pastor. Thank you for ruling with me.

In Him,

Johnny Young, Jr

-Note from the Author-

"The Word of God is the revealed

mind of God. The Body of Christ has been

held captive by

the religious doctrines and

traditions of men. Allow the scriptures to

do the speaking. Allow the words of the Father

to build faith. Possess the courage to

agree with God even

if it goes against the thing

you have been taught. You will never have the courage

to do until you first have

the courage to believe."

Johnny B. Young, Jr.

SECTION ONE:

THE TRUTH ABOUT YOUR IDENTITY

"Understanding Your Identity"

INTRODUCTION

Identity is important, but it is through purpose identity is revealed. When you know why a thing is you can discover what a thing is. Many believers are lost in identity because they are lost in purpose. Satan's greatest weapon is not sin, his greatest weapon is ignorance. Take a look at **Colossians 1:12-13**,

12. "Giving thanks unto the Father, which made us, meet (available) to be partakers of the inheritance of the saints in light. 13. Who hath delivered us from the power of darkness, and hath translated us into the kingdom of his dear son."

The word darkness in this scripture comes from the Greek word *sko-tos* and it means to cover or hide. Satan's kingdom is a kingdom of bondage. This bondage is based on lies and ignorance. If satan can keep you blind to the truth he can keep you in bondage. It is the revealed truth of God's word that causes you to be free.

"And you shall know the truth, and the truth shall make you free" **John 8:32**

We can see the powerful effect of ignorance in **Hosea 4:6**, "My people are destroyed for the lack of knowledge . . ."

Notice the cause of destruction was the lack of knowledge. Satan doesn't care about you being religious; he doesn't want you to gain knowledge of the truth. If the lack of knowledge can produce destruction then the acquisition of knowledge can cause a construction. In other words you can begin to experience growth and development in every area of your life when you gain knowledge of the truth, believe that truth and apply that truth.

In the body of Christ we have revelation on a lot of things. We know the purpose of praise and worship, we know the purpose of the tithes and offerings, we know the purpose of prayer but we have not majored in the subject of the purpose of man. We have kind of moved along with no real desire to know why I am here on earth?

When I am ignorant of the purpose of a thing I am sure to abuse that thing. The word abuse comes from two words Abnormal and Use and it means to improperly use in a hurtful way. When I am ignorant of my purpose and design I am sure to abuse my life. The objective of this book is to reveal that the bible speaks of three separate men; to expose their functions; and to reveal which man you are. The abuse stops now.

CHAPTER 1

The Dynamics of Man Let me begin by saying, Man is not an earth product. Man is a product of the unseen realm assigned to rule over the seen realm. It is imperative to understand that the bible actually speaks of three different men. We can see this in **1 Thessalonians 5:23**,

"And the very God of peace sanctify you wholly (completely); and I pray God your whole SPIRIT and SOUL and BODY be preserved blameless unto the coming of our Lord Jesus Christ.

Notice this scripture speaks of the spirit, soul and body are to be sanctified. The bible actually speaks of three different men and they are the spirit-man, the soul-man and the flesh-man. The key to living a kingdom purpose-filled life is see yourself the way God sees you and function in the way you were designed.

Now that we have revealed that there are actually three different men let us begin the journey of revealing which one you are. It is a common religious misconception to identify yourself to be all three of the men but you are not three men, you are one man. Which man am I? Am I spirit-man, soul-man or flesh-man? We can only seek the answer of this question in the word of God. Here is some advice, if you want to know what a thing is and why it exists never ask the thing. If you really want to know, just ask the one who made it. The identity of the thing and its purpose is found in the mind of its maker. So the identity and purpose of man is found in the mind of God our creator.

Am I Flesh-man?

The flesh-man is also known as the body (I like to call him the dirt-man). Since the flesh-man is often referred to as the body, let us look at some scriptures to see if we are the flesh-man.

"O wretched man that I am! Who shall deliver ME from THE BODY of this death?" **Romans 7:24**

The apostle Paul is writing of a war that is going on in His members. Notice that he says, who shall deliver ME from the BODY". This is a great point to know that if I am in bondage to the body then I cannot be the body. Paul said that the body or flesh-man had the real him in bondage. The body of Christ has been hindered in purpose because we have worked so hard to identify ourselves with the flesh-man. We preach sermons about the flesh-man, sing songs about the flesh-man and even pray flesh-led prayers right there at church. I am going to refer to a few more scriptures to further prove you are not your body or the flesh-man.

"I beseech you therefore, brethren, by the mercies of God, that YOU present YOUR BODIES a living sacrifice, holy and acceptable unto God, which is your reasonable service." **Romans 12:1**

You have to present your body; therefore you cannot be your body. This scripture separates YOU from YOUR BODY. You are not the flesh-man. Today is the day that you stop identifying yourself with the flesh and his weaknesses, shortcomings, or faults. You are not the flesh-man!

Am I the Soul-man?

Another common mistake is to identify ourselves with the soul. In scripture we can find the truth about ourselves. In **3 John 2** we see that we are not our souls.

"Beloved, I wish above all things that YOU may prosper and be in health, even as YOUR SOUL prospers."

The point is made clear here in this text that my soul is distinctively different from whom I am. In this scripture I am instructed to prosper as my soul prospers. If God tells me to prosper like David prospers, that would mean that David and I are two separate people. We cannot be the same person if we are to be in comparison to one another. The same is true concerning our identity. We are not the soul-man!

Am I the Spirit-man?

By process of elimination let me conclude that we are the spirit-man. However I am going to take the opportunity to prove it through scripture.

Hebrews 12:9, "Furthermore we have had fathers of our flesh which corrected us, and we gave them reverence: shall we not much rather be in subjection unto the father of SPIRITS and live?"

God is the father of spirit-men. To be a child of God means to be reborn spiritually. We are not reborn naturally or of our souls but we are reborn of our spirits. The real you is a spirit-man. Religions have majored in the subject of the flesh-man and education has mastered the advancement of the soul-man but little has been done to educate us concerning our true identity, spirit-man.

This is the true intended design and function of man in the earth realm representing the Kingdom of God enforcing its will in the earth. We have identified with the wrong men and it has cost a great deal. We have suffered in weakness and fear, wondering without purpose and direction because we didn't know the truth.

We can see God's design for man in the first two chapters of Genesis. His design is: Man is a Spirit who is housed in a body and he possesses a soul. He is not triune being. He is a Single, Whole being. He is not spirit, soul and body. He is a spirit-man that lives in a flesh-man while possessing a soul-man. Let us look at my favorite scripture in the bible which is **Genesis 1:26-27,**

26. "And God said, let us make man in our image, after our likeness and let them have dominion over the fish of the sea, and over the fowls of the air, and over the cattle, and over all the earth, and over every creeping thing that creepeth upon the earth. 27. So God creat-ED man in his own image . . ."

I love this passage of scripture, this is literally my favorite verse in the whole bible because it reveals the identity of man and purpose of man all in two scriptures. This is the first thing God said concerning man. We have advanced to want to do a lot of things for the Lord but we have not done the first thing yet.

God desired to have a man so he made a man in verse 26 and by verse 27 he is finished with the man. Notice in verse 27 the word create has an "ED" on it meaning it is past tense. By verse 27 man is created, it is done deal, past tense, finished. God created the real you (spirit-man) in **Genesis 1:26-27**. But we can see in Chapter 2 two other men are brought on the scene. The two other men are flesh-man and soul-man.

"And the Lord God formed man of the dust of the ground, and breathed into his nostrils the breath of life; and man became a living soul." **Genesis 2:7**

We see here that God formed man from the dust of the ground. Is this the same man in **Genesis 1:26**? No! The spirit-man is created and finished by **Genesis 1:27**, we see here another man is formed from the dust of the ground. This is the flesh-man. Church has identified themselves with this man for so long until you can ask any church member where do they come from and they will say from the dust of the ground. You do not come from the dust; the flesh-man that you are housed in comes from the dust.

There is a difference in your spirit-man and the flesh-man. We have reduced our worth and value because of the misconceptions religion taught us concerning these two scriptures.

God created a man in **Genesis 1:26-27** and then formed another man in **Genesis 2:7** and finally when He blew the man from chapter 1 into the man in chapter 2 the soul-man became active. If you are going to fulfill the will of God in the earth and properly re-present His kingdom He is going to need you to understand which man you are. You are not the flesh-man, you are not the soul-man you are the spirit-man. We must learn of our true identity. Each man has a specific design and function. If I don't learn their proper order I will function out of order.

CHAPTER 2

The Functions of the SPIRIT-MAN

I made a statement in the last chapter that I want to refer to right now: IF I
DON'T LEARN THE PROPER ORDER I WILL FUNCTION OUT OF ORDER.
This statement is true and powerful. God has created man with a specific order in
which we are designed to function and when man function out of that order it is
disaster.

Now that we know the bible speaks in reference to 3 different men and we know
which man we are, let us now learn concerning the functions of the Spirit-man (the
real you). Each man has an intended design and function. God created man with a
purpose. Remember identity is exposed by purpose. If I can know why a thing
exist, I can know what a thing is. We sometimes think we are on earth to wait until
Jesus come back so we can go to heaven. But Jesus said Father I pray that you
don't take them out of the world **(John 17:15).** We have been praying to leave
earth and Jesus prayed for us to stay to do what we were put here to do. We have
been taught that we are here on earth to give God praise, but God is not hurting for
praise, he has angels in heaven that are praising him continually. All of this sounds
good but they are not our purpose. We can find the purpose of man as we look at
His functions.

Here are the functions of the Spirit-man:

1. The Spirit-man is created to have dominion over the seen realm:

Look at **Genesis 1:26**, "And God said, let us make man in our image, after our likeness: and let them have DOMINION over the fish of the sea, and over the fowls of the air, and over the cattle, and OVER ALL THE EARTH, and over every creeping thing that creepeth upon the earth."

The Spirit-man that was created in Genesis 1:26-27 was created with the purpose of ruling over the seen realm. God wanted to extend his kingdom into the seen realm and he needs something to dominate or have dominion over all the earth. Something that would know his will and enforce His will in the earth. The purpose of which God created man is the identity of man. God wanted something to rule so he made a ruler! Look at it this way, He wanted something to fly so he made birds, He wanted something to swim so he made fish and he wanted something to govern, rule and dominate the whole earth so he made you! You were created with the purpose to have dominion over all the earth. If it is in the earth realm it is under your authority. Man's purpose of being created is to dominate or rule over the earth therefore man's identity is a dominator or ruler over the earth.

Genesis 9:2 (NLT) "All the animals of the earth, all the birds of the sky, all of the small animals that scurry along the ground, and all the fish in the sea will look on you with fear and terror. I HAVE PLACED THEM IN YOUR POWER"

Psalm 115:16, "The heavens, even the heavens, are the Lord's: but the earth hath He given to the children of men."

The real you is a ruler, created to enforce the will of God in the earth. You are created to have authority over every devil, demon sickness, disease and anything else in the earth. Adam was a spirit man having the very authority of God to enforce the rule of God but He lost this authority when he submitted to satan in sin (see **Genesis 3:1-10**).

Adam lost this authority but Jesus came to restore man to His purpose of dominion. You can see this in **Revelation 1:5-6**, " . . . Unto him that loved us, and WASHED US FROM OUR SINS IN HIS OWN BLOOD. And [he-Jesus] has made us KINGS and PRIEST unto God and his Father . . ."

Many believers believed Jesus died so they can go to heaven but this scripture tells us that He washed us in His blood to restore us to the original purpose of why we were created. We were created to enforce the will of God in the earth as rulers having dominion over all the earth and Jesus died to restore man to that position and purpose.

2. The spirit-man is created to be like God:

When God created the Spirit-man in **Genesis 1:26-27** He created the spirit-man in his own image and likeness. Many have a misinterpretation of this point. We have the ruined defeated mindset that we are useless no good, worthless sinners made of dirt but this is true concerning the flesh-man not the spirit-man. I am spirit-man and any man that has come to Jesus to trust Him as Lord and is born of the Spirit of God has been recreated or born again. This new nature is the original nature God had in man and that is the very nature of God.

Many have a low self-image of themselves because they confuse themselves with the flesh-man. I am not the flesh-man, I am the Spirit-man created to be like God. **Genesis 5:1 (NLT)** says, "This is the written account of the descendants of Adam. When God created human beings he made them TO BE LIKE HIMSELF . . ."

Religion has taught us that we are not like God and we will never be like God but God created us to be like himself.

To be like God means we have his:

- Speech: we talk like Him
- Thoughts: we think like Him
- Morals: we have the same standards. What is acceptable to Him is acceptable to me.
- Values: we value the same things. What is important to Him is important to me.
- Conduct: we have the same way of functioning.
- Character: we have the same nature

Kenneth E. Hagin wrote in his book Zoe: The God Kind Of Life (page 21) . . . "Eternal Life is the nature of God . . . I have the nature of God, the life of God, the wisdom of God". Today I make the same confession and any reborn person can make the same confession as well. This is powerful because you don't have to grow to become like God, you are recreated or reborn to be like God. You have His nature now. You don't have to wait until you get to Heaven to become like God. When He justified you he gave you His righteousness or nature. You are as righteous as you are ever going to be when you are born again. You may grow in holiness but you have His nature at the time of rebirth and you must know that you are just like God.

2 Corinthians 5:17-18 says, "Therefore if any man be in Christ, he is a new creature: old things are passed away; behold, all things are become new: And all things ARE OF GOD . . ."

So if any wrong thoughts or desires come to you, you can say, "these desires or thoughts are not my thoughts because I have the nature of God". Notice that verse 18 says everything that is in the new nature (the spirit-man) is of God. You have the very nature of God, so any thought that is not like God did not originate in you (spirit-man). You can now cast down alien thoughts, habits and desires that are not like God. They are the thoughts, desires and habits of another man trying to push them on you to believe and act out.

3. The Spirit-man receives information from the Holy Spirit.

The Holy Spirit is sent to teach us concerning who we are and what we are created to do. He receives from Jesus and reveals to us (See **John 16:13-14**). When the Holy Spirit speaks he only speaks to spirit-man. He never speaks to the flesh or the soul-man. It is his desire to communicate with you (spirit-man).

Romans 8:16 says, "The [Holy] Spirit itself bears witness (or communicate) with our spirit, that we are children of God."

The pattern is the Holy Spirit reveals the mind of Christ to you that you can function with the mind of Christ. He teaches, guides, leads and instructs us in righteousness. The real you receives the life and truth of Holy Spirit. The spirit-man looks to the truth of God's word only. It never looks to the earth for knowledge, help or support. You must know that your function as spirit-man is to receive information from the Holy Spirit and enforce that information in the earth with all authority. This is why you seek truth because you are a truth seeker and the Holy Spirit is the Spirit of truth.

CHAPTER 3

The Functions of the SOUL-MAN

" . . . and man became a living soul . . ." **Genesis 2:7**

As I stated earlier the real you which is spirit-man was created in **Genesis 1:26-27**. Then in **Genesis 2:7** God formed another man from the ground for you to live in (flesh man) and blew you and the soul into the flesh-man. The purpose of the soul is very important. Although you have been born again or recreated if you do nothing to your soul you will not be able to live out that new birth experience.

What is the Soul?

Many times when the bible is speaking of the soul it uses the word heart but it is really making reference to the spirit. To fully understand the scriptures one must be able to understand what man God is making reference to at what time. However, the soul is vitally important to living out the kingdom mandate in the earth. The soul is the seat for the mind and emotions. It is the place for the thoughts and the feelings.

Here are the functions of the Soul:

1. The soul-man was created to have feelings (emotions) and thoughts:

David made reference to His soul in **Psalm 42:5** where He said, "Why are you cast down, 0 my soul? And why are you disquieted in me? Hope thou in God: for 1 shall praise him for the help of His countenance."

I love this scripture because first of all David realizes that he is not his soul. He confronts the feelings of his soul and commands the soul to hope thou in God. Many believers miss it right here. They don't understand that feelings take place in the soulish-man and they identify themselves with that man.

I serve as the overseer of Heavenly Hope Ministries in Baton Rouge, La and as a Pastor I have the opportunity to counsel many people. There are times when someone wants to get married because they FEEL like they love the person and when I learn of their feelings I tell them love is not a feeling. According to **Galatians 5:22**, it is an activity of the Holy Spirit reproducing the nature of God in the spirit man. It has nothing to do with feelings. Many people are led by their feelings or even controlled by their feelings. I have seen couples who have been married for over 15 years get a divorce because they were led by their feelings. Believers leave church, quit jobs and leave assignments because of the feelings of the soul. I like to say they are soulish because they are easily offended and sensitive about any and everything. Paul wrote of the importance of the soul in **1 Thessalonians 5:23**, " . . . I pray God that your WHOLE spirit and SOUL… be preserved blameless . . ."

Many believers come to the altar and embrace Jesus as Lord and are even filled with the Holy Spirit and expect to see change and they have yet to do anything to their soul-man. Paul said in **Romans 12:2**, "and be not conformed to this world: but be transformed by the renewing of your mind (soul man), that you may prove [experience] what is the good, and acceptable, and perfect, will of God."

This verse tells us that we will be transformed as we renew our mind (soul-man) and then I can experience the will of God for my life. We renew our minds with the word of God. A new spirit-man and an un-renewed soul-man are fruitless. When Adam fell into sin he fell from a place of unhindered union with God. He fell from the spirit realm into the soulish realm of being controlled by his feelings and led of natural knowledge. The soul gains what is called acquired knowledge. He takes in whatever he can grab hold on to whether it is from the spirit man or the flesh man.

2. The Soul-man is created to be a messenger:

You may be asking how is the soul a messenger. The purpose or plan of God for the soul is to be the man that connects the spirit-man to the flesh-man. The spirit-man is created to be like God, receive information from the Holy Spirit and dominate the whole earth and He is housed in the earthly house or he lives in the flesh-man. The soul-man is created to relay information from the spirit-man to the flesh-man. He never presents his own thoughts. Everything he knows he either received it from the spirit-man or the flesh-man.

The soul stores up knowledge. It gathers as much knowledge as possible and stores it up. It either receives revealed knowledge from the spirit-man or it receives reserved knowledge from the flesh man. This is what strongholds are; they are experiences that are stored up in the soul.

The intended function for the soul is to receive information from the spirit man and relay that information to the flesh man. But when Adam sinned this order was perverted and the flesh man began to send messages through the soul to the spirit man who was too weak to take authority because he was cut off from God.

I see soulish believers all the time. When it is time to worship they don't worship because they don't FEEL like worshipping or they don't come to church because they don't FEEL like coming. They are offended by something somebody did and refuse to forgive and let it go. The soul was never created to rule you. When you hear the soul man telling you how he feels you should do like David in **Psalm 42:5** and that is confront your soul and command it to line up. When you see a stronghold that have been built up in your soul you're to confront, cast it down and command the soul to line up with the Word of God. Don't allow your soul to rule.

God never gave dominion to your soul man, he gave dominion to you! You are the dominator, you are the ruler, you are the authority and as you receive information from the Holy Ghost you command your soul to relay that information to your flesh.

Some of us have been living under the rule of the soul for so long until it is a real battle to break free. **Hebrews 4:12** says, "For the word of God is quick [alive and active], and powerful, and sharper than any two edged sword, piercing even to the dividing asunder of the SOUL and SPIRIT . . ."

The only thing that can cut you away from the dictations of the soul is the word of God. Application of the word cuts the real you (spirit man) away from the soul man. You are the authority, the soul is the messenger. If you don't rule it, it will rule you, and lead you around helplessly. You are created to be Spirit-Led not Sense-ruled. Reason is an activity of the soul but faith is an activity of the spirit man.

You cannot afford to ignore the need to rule your soul by applying the word of God. The soul was created to relay information from the spirit man to the flesh man. So when the soul presents a thought or desire you are to cast it down and tell the soul I have authority over you and you are to relay the information I give you not the information you receive from the flesh man. For instance the words of the Doctor comes through your ear (apart of the flesh man) into your soul and when your soul tries to get you to believe that word from the doctor you are to cast it down and take authority over your soul and relay the word you (spirit man) received from the Holy Spirit and tell the soul to tell the flesh we will believe the word of God and not the word of the doctors. This is the proper order and function of man.

CHAPTER 4

The Functions of the FLESH-MAN

I first started with the statement that Man is not an earth product. Man is a product of the unseen realm assigned to rule over the seen realm. We have embraced the religious misconception that we are dirt-men so long until we have such a low esteem of ourselves. You did not come from the earth, you came from God (**Genesis 1:26-27**), the flesh-man or the house you live in came from the dust of the ground (**Genesis 2:7**). Just like the Spirit-man or the Soul-man the Flesh-man has purpose as well.

1. The flesh-man is created to be your connection to the seen realm:

Every kingdom seeks to expand and extended its kingdom into new territory. This process is called colonization. God's Kingdom is the same. God created an earth because He had a desire for His kingdom to extend from heaven into the earth. His plan was for them both to function to under the same government and for earth to be a mirror reflection of what heaven is.

Look at the prayer of Jesus in **Matthew 6:9-10**, " . . . Our father which art in heaven, Hallowed be thy name. 10. Thy Kingdom come. Thy will be done in earth AS IT IS in heaven . . ."

Jesus prayed for whatever is going on in heaven to be going in the earth. This is the ultimate plan of God, to extend His kingdom into the earth (for more on this subject retrieve the messages Understanding the Kingdom and Embracing the Kingdom). However, the plan of God to extend His kingdom from the unseen realm would cause for a regent or ruler in the seen realm. It would have to be somebody with His mind, character, morals, values and ability. It would have to be somebody like him and they would have to live, function and enforce His will in the seen realm of the earth. So after the Lord made the earth he created a ruler for the territory. A ruler that was like him, a ruler that had his mind, character and ability by way of the Holy Spirit. This ruler was man (spirit-man). So in **Genesis 2:7** we see the first function of the flesh-man in action. God takes the spirit-man and blows him into the flesh-man. For the spirit-man to function, live and operate in the earth he would need an earthly body to function through.

Every spirit including God is limited to what they can do in the earth realm without a body. This is seen in **Luke 11:24 (NLT)**, "When an evil spirit leaves a person (or body), it goes into the desert, SEARCHING FOR REST. But when it finds none, it says, I will return to the person I came from."

Satan understands that he can only function in the earth through an available body. God himself is limited to what he can do in the earth without a body. I know it is hard to believe that God would be limited because religion filled us up with so much junk but God is in need of an available body to function in the earth.

2 Chronicles 16:9 talks about how God is searching the whole earth for a person that will give him access into the earth.

2 Timothy 2:21 tells us God's plan to use man as a vessel or avenue to work in the earth. Let's say it this way; if satan wanted to hit me he would need a body to use their hand. If satan wanted to kick me, he would need a body to use their feet. If satan wanted to curse me, he would need a body to use their mouth. God is the same way; He needs a body to function in the earth. This why God always keep a remnant of believers in the earth that He can always have access into the earth to show himself strong. You are the same way. You were created a spirit-man but to function in the earth God had to put in the earth suit or a flesh body. This would make you legal to function in the seen realm as you function through a seen body.

The Importance of the Flesh-man

This is why taking care of your body is important because without your body you are no longer legal to function in the earth. Misuse and neglect of your body can lead to early departure from the earth. This is why Jesus came down and took on an earthly fleshly body because it would give him access into the earth realm to restore the fallen man. It was a spirit man who was housed in a fleshly body that gave away to satan the authority over the earth and it would take the same to take it back.

2. The Flesh-man is created to act out the instructions of the Spirit-man.

The Flesh-man was created to receive instructions from the spirit man through the soul and then act out those instructions in the earth. When Adam sinned, this whole process was perverted. The spirit-man died and withered as the Holy Spirit departed and the flesh man then took on the nature of satan and submitted to his rule. Satan then began to rule over your flesh causing your flesh to be dominant and controlling.

The flesh-man then began to promote his thoughts and desires; and the soul instead of relaying from the spirit to the flesh began to relay from the flesh to the spirit. The flesh was created to act out the instructions of the Holy Spirit. The spirit-man would receive information from the Holy Spirit and then issue a command to the soul-man; the soul-man would then relay that information to the flesh and what God said to the spirit-man would then be displayed through the flesh-man acting on the Word of God.

I am created to have dominion over the flesh-man. Paul wrote in **Romans 12:1**, " . . . that you [spirit-man] (are to) present your bodies (or flesh-man) a living sacrifice . . ."

Paul also wrote in **1 Thessalonians 4:4 (NLT)**, "Then each of you will control [rule, dominate] his own body (or Flesh-man) . . ."

He also writes in **1 Corinthians 9:27 (NLT)**, "I [spirit-man] discipline my body [flesh-man] like an athlete, training it [flesh-man] to do what it should . . ."

In these scriptures Paul reveals a wonderful truth and that truth is God is not going to rule your flesh. **Genesis 2:7** says that your flesh comes from the earth. It is earthly material; it is an earth product and **Genesis 1:26** states that God gave you dominion over the earth. If you [spirit-man] have authority over the earth and your flesh is from the earth then you are in charge to rule over your flesh. Notice Paul says YOU must present your body, YOU must possess your body, YOU must discipline your body and YOU must train your body to function in order and not allow it to run out of order. The body or the flesh-man is under your command and authority. Rule it or it will rule you.

Your flesh has purpose and its purpose is to connect you [spirit-man] to the seen realm and act out the instructions of the spirit-man. He is valuable in his purpose but when you allow him to do the leading, ruling and controlling; when you allow him to present his desires and thoughts without correcting him and putting him back in place you will find yourself in bondage physically, mentally and spiritually.

CHAPTER 5

The Right way to Function

Let us begin this chapter with the opening statement: Man is not an earth product. Man is a product of the unseen realm assigned to rule over the seen realm. It was never God's plan to have servants, slaves, church folks or religious groups but His plan was always to have a kingdom that would extend into the earth and His sons created in His image and likeness, possessing his nature, mind and ability, filled with His Spirit would rule the earth and promote, present, and enforce the rule of God in the earth. We have the responsibility of making earth look just like heaven. Many find this hard to believe and they even think it is impossible because they have identified themselves with the flesh-man instead of their true identity, spirit-man. God never wanted religious followers, he wanted royal leaders.

To function in our purpose and Kingdom assignment we must identify ourselves as the spirit-man created to be like God in every way, created to have dominion over all the earth, and created to receive instruction and information from the Holy Spirit. We must release the grip of the misconceptions of thinking we are the soul-man and flesh-man because they are servants created to serve you (spirit-man) and then you are to cause the will (morals, power, wisdom and character) of God to be made visible in the earth.

This improper view of the identity of man has brought great damage to the mindset of man. Much credit to this damage goes to religion. Religion is God's greatest enemy because it is the soul's or flesh's attempt to please God while being ignorant or rebellious to the proper order of man.

IT WAS NEVER GOD'S DESIRE TO RULE THE EARTH. Let us look at a few scriptures to solidify this point:

Genesis 1:26, "And God said, Let us make man in our image and after our likeness: and let them have dominion . . . over all the earth".

Psalm 8:6, "Thou has made him [man / spirit-man] to have dominion over the works of thy hands, thou past put ALL THINGS UNDER HIS FEET:"

Psalm 116:15-16, "You are blessed of the Lord which made heaven and earth. The heaven, even the heavens, are the Lord's: BUT THE EARTH HE HAS GIVEN TO THE CHILDREN OF MEN."

Once again I state it was never God's will to rule the earth. His desire was different. Let me express his desire,

> *"He desired to rule the seen from the unseen by the unseen living
> in the seen on the scene."*

Dr. Myles Munroe (Rediscovering the Kingdom)

No! He never wanted to rule the earth.

"He desired to rule the seen (earth realm) from the Unseen

(heavenly realm) by the unseen (spirit-man filled with the Holy

Spirit) living in the seen (flesh-man) on the scene."

So you see we hold up the plan of God when we function out-side of our purpose. As long as you think you are the flesh-man you will always be weak and defeated. God gave authority and dominion to the spirit-man in **Genesis 1:26** not the flesh-man. The only thing he gave the flesh-man was instructions to work (see **Genesis 2:15-17**).

The neglect of teaching concerning your true identity as stated earlier has caused great damage. You have gone through life acting like the flesh-man because you don't know the real you. For instance, let us look at **Matthew 26:41**, "Watch and pray, that you enter not into temptation: for the spirit is willing, but the flesh is weak."

We have allowed the misconception of this scripture to circulate in the church for too long. We have used this as a scripture to excuse the behavior of the flesh. I was ministering to a guy one day and he was telling me how he wanted to stop smoking cigarettes, so I told him, "oh that's easy, just stop". He said, "Bishop Young, it's not that easy", so I said, "brother it is easy, I guarantee if you put your cigarettes down they will not jump in your mouth". He then said (in a very religious tone),

"Bishop Young, the spirit is willing but you know the flesh is weak". I told him, "You are the spirit not the flesh".

This scripture is revealing our true identity, we have always view ourselves as the weak flesh in this scripture but you are the willing spirit not the weak flesh. I told the brother, "you are the one that is willing to quit smoking but the flesh-man is too weak to quit on his own". We must understand that I am the willing one not the weak one. I am the one that is willing to love, believe, give, worship or anything else the word of God commands me.

If I am going to identify with the flesh then I will always make excuses to not act on the word of God because the flesh is weak (he has no dominion or authority). If I never learn about me (spirit-man) I will always act like him (flesh-man).

There is a story I like to tell of an eagle's egg that fell down into a chicken yard and the mother hen gathered the egg and sat on it until it hatched. The egg hatched and the mother hen raised the little eagle with the rest of the little chickens. So the eagle is walking through the yard acting just like a chicken because it was raised and trained to think it was one, until one day they saw this beautiful bird flying high in the sky. The little eagle turned to the mother hen and asked what kind of bird is that. The mother eagle said, that is the birds of all birds, that is the eagle but don't worry, you will never be like that. Sad to say but that little eagle died thinking it was a chicken. Many believers have longed within to be more, to do more and have died thinking they was less than what they really were.

Each man (spirit, soul and flesh) have their own desires. The spirit-man always has the desires of God.

Galatians 5:22-23 reveals those desires, it says, "But the fruit of the Spirit is love, joy, peace, longsuffering, gentleness, goodness, faith, meekness, temperance . . . ."

Colossians 3:10 (NLT), "Put on the new nature (reborn spirit-man), and he renewed (mentally) as you learn to know your creator and become like him."

Ephesians 4:20-24 (NLT), "But that isn't what you learned about Christ. Since you have heard about Jesus and have learned the truth that comes from Him, throw off your old sinful nature (the nature of the flesh-man) and you former way of life, which is corrupted by lust and deception. Instead, let the Spirit renew your thoughts and attitudes. Put on the new nature (reborn spirit-man) created to be like God-truly righteous and holy. You can see the desires of the flesh-man in the following scriptures:

Romans 7:18, "For I know that in me (that is, in my flesh,) dwelleth no good thing: for to will is present with me; but how to perform that which is good I find not."

1 Peter 2:11, "Dearly beloved, I beseech you as strangers and pilgrims, abstain from fleshly lusts, which war against the soul;"

James 1:13-14, "Let no man say when he is tempted, I am tempted of God: for God cannot be tempted with evil, neither tempteth he any man: But every man is tempted, when he is drawn away of his own lust, and enticed."

1 John 2:16, "For all that is in the world, the lust of the flesh, and the lust of the eyes, and the pride of life, is not of the Father, but is of the world"

1 Corinthians 6:9-11, "Know ye not that the unrighteous shall not inherit the kingdom of God? Be not deceived: neither fornicators, nor idolaters, nor adulterers, nor effeminate, nor abusers of themselves with mankind, Nor thieves, nor covetous, nor drunkards, nor revilers, nor extortioners, shall inherit the kingdom of God."

Galatians 5:19-21, "Now the works of the flesh are manifest, which are these; Adultery, fornication, uncleanness, lasciviousness, Idolatry, witchcraft, hatred, variance, emulations, wrath, strife, seditions, heresies, Envyings, murders, drunkenness, revellings, and such like: of the which I tell you before, as I have also told you in time past, that they which do such things shall not inherit the kingdom of God."

Colossians 3:5-9 (AMP), "So kill (deaden, deprive of power) the evil desire lurking in your members [those animal impulses and all that is earthly in you that is employed in sin]: sexual vice, impurity, sensual appetites, unholy desires, and all greed and covetousness, for that is idolatry (the deifying of self and other created things instead of God). It is on account of these [very sins] that the [holy] anger of God is ever coming upon the sons of disobedience (those who are obstinately opposed to the divine will), Among whom you also once walked, when you were living in and addicted to [such practices]. But now put away and rid yourselves [completely] of all these things: anger, rage, bad feeling toward others, curses and slander, and foulmouthed abuse and shameful utterances from your lips! Do not lie to one another, for you have stripped off the old (unregenerate) self with its evil practices,"

These desires are enemies to the spirit-man and are in complete contrast to the will of God. The desires of the flesh are deadly, they are an enemy to all that you are. Every time the flesh speaks or presents a desire or thought it is for your destruction. He is trying to kill me and strip me of my eternal promise, royal identity, fellowship with the King, elevated position of authority, divine assignment and purpose. I am not my flesh! Therefore, I must separate my identity from the desires, thoughts and will of the flesh. The desires of the spirit-man are always the opposite of the desires of the flesh (see **Galatians 5:17**). When I know the desires of each man I can know what man is speaking at what time. I will not experience true Kingdom Living until I (spirit-man) receive the information and instruction of the Holy Spirit and then I take my position of authority and put the other men in check (soul and flesh-man).

The flesh is habit forming or addictive by nature. Whether it is food, fun, exercise or etc, if you do anything long enough it will become addictive to your flesh. The flesh will never volunteer to do the will of God. He must be forced or dominated. He has to be crucified and brought under subjection daily.

1 Corinthians 9:27, "But I keep under my body, and bring it into subjection: lest that by any means, when I have preached to others, I myself should be a castaway."

Romans 13:14, "But put ye on the Lord Jesus Christ, and make not provision for the flesh, to fulfil the lusts thereof."

So when the flesh tries to rule put him in his place by the power of the Holy Ghost and when the soul presents how he feels you tell him, "I am the one who gives you commands and refuse to allow you to give me commands". When the flesh presents an ungodly thought or desire, exercise authority over him and tell him," you will do what I command you to do".

The Holy Spirit lives in you to empower you, instruct you, inform you, teach you and prepare you to be the man God created you to be. The Word of God is the tool the Holy Spirit uses to release and retrain me to function in the spirit. Give place to the Word. This is your kingdom design. You are the willing one, not the weak one!

Live the way you are designed to live and watch the promises of God manifest in your life like never before.

SECTION TWO:

THE TRUTH ABOUT YOUR POSITION

"Developing the ways of Royalty"

CHAPTER 6

Introduction to Royalty

That is why your land is mourning, and everyone is wasting away. Even the wild animals, the birds of the sky and the fish of the sea are disappearing. My people are being destroyed because they don't know me . . ." **Hosea 4:3, 6**

The earth is suffering! Suffering from violence and abuse of every kind. Suffering from the ideologies and misconceptions of the traditions of men. Suffering from the damaging effects of religion. Muslims, Buddhists, Hindus and even Christians have caused much damage to the hearts and minds of many.

All of the earth is covered with chaos and the whole world is looking for results. In this time and hour religion is falling apart at its hinges because religion will only promise, "it will get better later". It doesn't have the ability to give results, bring change or provide solutions to the realities of right now. The Kingdom of God has been misrepresented by religious followers who are actually working against the plan of God in the name of God.

The plan of God was never to establish a religion. His plan was to establish His Kingdom in the earth. A kingdom that lives above the limitations of the earth. A kingdom of power, wisdom, strength and glory. A kingdom of solutions!

Jesus clearly stated that His purpose in His earthly ministry was a Kingdom assignment. **Luke 4:43**, " . . . I must preach the good news of the Kingdom of God in other towns too, BECAUSE THAT IS WHY I WAS SENT". God's plan is for the government of Heaven to influence the earth until the earth is filled with His characteristics, principles and power. To do this the King redeemed His children and filled them with His Spirit that they will function, think, speak, have the power and live like the King in the earth. Since God is a King and we are His kids, that makes us ROYALTY. THIS IS OUR POSITION IN CHRIST! As Sons of the King we are filled the wisdom, power and authority of the King to bring Kingdom solutions to all the earthly problems. All of creation is waiting on the real you to show up. Don't keep them waiting.

"For the earnest expectation of the creature waiteth for the manifestation of the sons of God" **Romans 8:19**

Chapter 7

Ignorant Rulers

As stated earlier, God never wanted to start a religion. He never wanted to create a denomination. He wanted to establish His Kingdom on earth. He didn't want religious followers, He wanted royal leaders. He wanted sons to rule in the earth in His name.

John 15:15, "I no longer call you servants . . ."

Galatians 4:7, "Wherefore thou art no more a servant, but a son; and if a son, then an heir of God through Christ."

Religion has conditioned the minds of believers to be servants, when God has clearly stated we are no more servants but sons. WE ARE ROYALTY!

God has made every effort for us to be royalty. The word Royalty means—the regal elevated position of authority. Royalty always deals with authority. You will never have royalty without authority. Religion is working to keep you ignorant of your position as a son. In fact religion killed the first son our King Jesus Christ not because of his miracles or power. They killed Him because he said He was a Son (see **John 19:6-7**). Religion will fight to keep you from being the royal son that you are.

There are (5) roads to becoming Royal

1. *Creation*: This when you were created to be in the position of authority.
2. *Birth*: This when a King or Royal official gives birth to a child and that child is automatically royal through birth.

This can be seen in the life of Solomon. David was King and when he had a son (Solomon) his son automatically became a ROYAL prince.

3. *Delegation*: This is when a Ruler or person in the position of authority appoints or gives power to another for the purpose of ruling or managing.

I don't think there is a more vivid example of becoming royal through delegation than in the life Joseph. In **Genesis 41:37-44** we see delegation at work. God used Joseph to interpret the Pharaoh's dream and bring solutions to the problem of an upcoming famine (recession). The Pharaoh took the ring off his finger and put it on Joseph's hand and publicly delegated authority to Joseph and at that point Joseph went from the prison to the palace. He went, from being a servant and a prisoner to being a ruler all because He was delegated authority.

4. *Marriage*: This is when a person of Royalty marries a another person, thus making them royal through marriage.

There is a clear example ((becoming royal through marriage in **Esther 2:1-17** where there was a slave girl who became the Royal Queen because she married the King.

5. _Adoption_: This is when a person of Royalty adopts or takes in a child to as their own child making the child royal.

For an example of this road to royalty we can search the scriptures and look at **Exodus 2:1-10**. Moses was sent up the river to escape death and the Pharaoh's daughter (the princess) found him and adopted him making Moses a royal ruler in Egypt.

So the (5) roads to royalty are: _Creation, Birth, Delegation, Marriage_ and _Adoption_. Our Father covered every road to us being royal. We therefore have no excuse for not ruling.

A. We are <u>CREATED</u> to rule with authority

"And God said, Let us make man in our image, after our likeness: and let them have dominion over the fish of the sea, and over the fowl of the air, and over the cattle, AND OVER ALL THE EARTH, and over everything that creepeth upon the earth." **Genesis 1:26 (KJV)**

B. We are <u>BORN</u> into the family of God through the rebirth of the Spirit to rule with authority.

"For whatsoever is Born of God overcometh the world: and this is the victory that overcometh the world, even our faith." **1 John 5:4**

C. We have been <u>DELEGATED</u> authority to rule by our King Jesus Christ.

"Behold! I have given you authority and power to trample upon serpents and scorpions, and [physical and mental strength and ability] over all the power that the enemy [possess]; and nothing shall in any way harm you." **Luke 10:19 (Amplified)**

D. We are <u>MARRIED</u> to the King Jesus Christ to rule with authority.

"For thy maker is your husband: the Lord of host is his name . . ." **Isaiah 54:5 (KJV)**

E. We are <u>ADOPTED</u> into the family of God to rule with authority.

"To redeem them that were under the law, that we might receive the adoption of sons." **Galatians 4:5**

Notice that the reoccurring theme is our King is making sure that we have authority to RULE over all the earth in His name to establish His Kingdom and enforce His will in the earth.

There are (10) synoptic words that run parallel with the word RULE.

1. *Reign* - to be the top authority in a particular territory.
2. *Dominate* - to express or show the power and authority of being over a place or thing.
3. *Lead* - to go before and expose to others the way by example.

4. _Conquer_ - to overthrow opposing power and forces and establish the rule of another.

5. _Subdue_ - to eliminate any and everything that is a threat to your rule.

6. _Govern_ - to manage or be responsible for the affairs in a particular territory.

7. _Instruct_ - to teach, command, explain or demonstrate the proper way of function, activity or conduct.

8. _Direct_ - to give guidance with great wisdom and knowledge.

9. _Control_ - to influence a territory with force, threat or mental ability.

10. _Believe_ - to have authority over your (5) senses, intellectual reason or emotions.

God says you are royalty but satan has hid this truth from you through misconceptions and lies. Religion tells us we are to wait to rule later in heaven but God says we are rulers now!

1 John 4:17, " . . . but we can face him with confidence because we live like Jesus here in this world."

We were created, born, delegated, married and adopted to rule, reign, dominate, lead, conquer, subdue, govern, instruct, direct, control and believe in the name of our King. When we are ignorant of our position of authority everything that we are to rule over will rule us. TO BE ANYTHING OTHER THAN A RULER AND TO DO ANYTHING OTHER THAN RULE IS TO BE OUT OF THE WILL OF GOD.

Ecclesiastes 10:5, 7, "There is an evil which I have seen under the sun, as an error which proceedeth from the ruler. I have seen servants upon horses (like rulers) and princes (rulers) walking as servants upon the earth.

You are royalty. You are a ruler and now is the time to allow the Holy Spirit to Develop in you the ways of Royalty.

"Then Samuel explains to the people the ways of Royalty . . . **1 Samuel 10:25 (NKJV)**

CHAPTER 8

Royalty Commands

Where the word of a king is, there is power: and who may say unto him, What doest thou?" **Ecclesiastes 8:4**

I am intrigue with the royal court of England. The Queen of England has (2) grandsons Prince William and Prince Harry. From their birth up until this present moment tutors and governors have been training them in the ways of royalty. Personal assistants travel with them everywhere they go to guide, instruct and develop them to function, think and speak in the Royal Way. They are not average kids, they are Royalty. They are in the elevated position of authority.

Likewise, we have a Governor or Personal Helper called the Holy Spirit who is with us everywhere we go and he is guiding, instructing and developing in us the ways of the Kingdom of God. Although we are in this earth we are not average people, we are children of the King of Glory. We are in the elevated position of authority. The first thing we need to understand about the ways of Royalty is, Royalty always commands. We have established the fact that we are in the elevated position of authority to establish the rule of the Kingdom of God and enforce that rule in the earth.

"For verily I say unto you, That whosoever shall say unto this mountain, Be thou removed, and be thou cast into the sea; and shall not doubt in his heart, but shall BELIEVE THAT THOSE THINGS WHICH HE SAITH shall come to pass; he shall have whatsoever HE SAITH." **Mark 11:23 (KJV)**

"And the Lord said, If ye had faith as a grain of mustard seed, ye might SAY unto this sycamine tree, Be thou plucked up by the root, and be thou planted in the sea, and IT SHOULD OBEY YOU." **Luke 17:6 (KJV)**

We are aware that things obey God when He speaks but we are have little to no confidence in the words we speak and it is because we don't understand the ways of Royalty. Everything under your rule, servants seen and unseen go to work to bring to pass the words that come out of your mouth.

Another example of the power of the command of royalty is in **2 Samuel 23:13-17 (Message Translation)**

13-17 One day during harvest, the Three parted from the Thirty and joined David at the Cave of Adullam. A squad of Philistines had set up camp in the Valley of Rephaim. While David was holed up in the Cave, the Philistines had their base camp in Bethlehem. **David had a sudden craving and SAID**, *"Would I ever like a drink of water from the well at the gate of Bethlehem!"* <u>**So the Three penetrated the Philistine lines, drew water from the well at the gate of Bethlehem**</u>, *and brought it back to David. But David wouldn't drink it; he poured it out as an offering to God, saying, "There is no way, God, that I'll drink this! This isn't mere* *water, it's their life-blood—they risked their very lives to bring it!" So David refused to drink it. This is the sort of thing that the Three did.*

Pay close attention it wasn't WHAT David said, it was the fact that HE (*the position of* authority) SAID and they heard it as a command. We must understand that like David when we speak our words are heard as commands and every angel and earthly element moves to bring to pass what we say.

Let's look at another example, "When Jesus returned to Capernaum, a roman officer came and pleaded with him. Lord, my young servant lies in bed, paralyzed and in terrible pain. Jesus said, I will come and heal him. But the officer said, Lord I am not worthy to have you come into my home. Just SAY the word from where you are, and my servant will be healed. I know because I am under authority of my superior officers and I HAVE AUTHORITY OVER MY SOLDIERS. I ONLY NEED TO SAY, go and they go or come and they come . . ." **Matthew 8:5-9**

This passage of scriptures serve as an awesome testimony to the fact the Royalty are commanders. The centurion was able to have great faith because he understood authority. He understood that authority always flow down. Authority never flows upward. The student never has authority over the teacher, or the employee never has authority over the employer, neither do subjects command kings. If the person in authority speaks everything under his authority moves to carry out what they have said. The authority is released in the words and the words the commands are issued.

Jesus when he was on trial before Pilate, falsely imprisoned by the Jewish council he refused to respond to the questions or insults surrounding him. Jesus at this point has chosen to be silent and he refused to speak because he was on a mission and this mission required that he give his life for all of mankind. He refused to speak because Jesus knew that as long as there was a word coming out of His mouth he would never be handed over to be put to death. In essence, Jesus had to shut up to die! The point that I am making is, we cannot afford to be silent. If we shut up, we will die!

If you are not satisfied with the conditions of your life in any area open your mouth and issue a command. Seen and unseen servants are waiting to carry out your next command.

Proverbs 18:20 says,

(KJV) A man's belly shall be SATISFIED with the fruit his mouth; and with the increase of his lips shall he be filled.

(NLT) "Wise words satisfy like a good meal; the right words bring satisfaction."

If there is any area in your life where you are not satisfied, the royal thing to do is to issue a command in that area of your life. The right words will bring satisfaction.

CHAPTER 9

Royalty is Never Fearful but Always Courageous

- **Courageous** - *to be fearless or refusing to be intimidated in the face of trial, danger or opposition.*

God can do very little with a fearful believer. Fear is an instrument of the enemy. Fear paralyzes you and gives the devil access into your life. Courage is the opposite. Courage is the byproduct of faith and confidence. With faith you will courageously accomplish great things.

"By faith these people overthrew kingdoms, ruled with justice, and received what God had promised them. They shut the mouths of lions, quenched the flames of fire, and escaped death by the edge of the sword. Their weakness was turned to strength. They became strong in battle and put whole armies to flight . . ."
Hebrews 11:33-34

Courage is the way of royalty. Only the courageous are able to function in the elevated position of authority. The body of Christ has everything we need to live victorious lives but there is one problem. Majority of believers are so easily intimidated.

They are fearful and intimidated by any and everything. Swine flu, the state of the economy, natural disasters, sickness and disease, predators of all kind and everything else cause most believers to shrink in fear instead of standing in faith and courage. As believers we have a promise from our King to protect us from swine flu or any other plague.

"no evil will conquer you and no plague will near you home." **Psalm 91:10**

We have a promise from our King to protect us from the falling, failing economy in **Philippians 4:19**. We have promises to believe and principles to apply that will give us victory against every problem we face in the earth if we will not coward back in fear but stand firm in faith with courage.

Let us look at the life of Job. He was a perfect and upright man who feared God and shunned evil. One day Job lost his children, homes, cattle, health and he almost lost his marriage. This was a horrible series of events. Talk about having a bad day. If we look in the first chapter we would see that the Lord allowed the enemy to bring on these catastrophic events in Job's life (Job 1-2). Although God didn't do it, he gave satan permission to do so. Why? We can find Job's folly in Job 3:25, "For the thing which I greatly feared is come upon me, and that which I was afraid of is come unto me.

You see although Job loved God he still had fear hidden in him. So God orchestrated a plan to cause Job to courageously face his fears instead of running from them. God used satan to help get the infection of fear out of Job. Glory to God! He will allow satan to operate in the plan but not plan the operation.

Likewise, God is working to remove the damaging infectious seed of fear in you that the royal courageous ruler you are will stand and act in faith with boldness.

Let us look at how intensely God desires to develop the courageous character of royalty in you by looking at the life of Joshua.

"After the death of Moses the Lord's servant, the LORD spoke to Joshua son of Nun, Moses' assistant. He said, Moses my servant is dead. Therefore, the time has come for you to lead these people, the Israelites, across the Jordan River into the land I am giving them. I promise you what I have promised Moses: Wherever you set foot, you will be on land I have given you. No one will be able to stand against you as long as you live. For I will be with you as I was with Moses. I will not fail you or abandon you. Be strong and courageous for you are the one who will lead these people to possess all the land I swore to their ancestors I would give them. Be strong and very courageous . . . Study this book of Instruction continually. meditate on it day and night so you will be sure to obey everything written in it. Only then will you prosper and succeed in all you do. This is my command—Be strong and courageous! Do not be afraid or discouraged. For the LORD your God is with you wherever you go." **Joshua 1:1-3, 5-8**

Joshua was Moses' successor and he was delegated authority to lead (rule) the children of Israel as they entered into the promised land. This was a big responsibility and the message from the LORD to Joshua was to "BE STRONG AND VERY COURAGEOUS". What the Lord was telling Joshua is the same thing He is telling you. If you are going to rule, if you are going to lead, you must understand on this journey you will face many oppositions, many enemies and many turbulent situations but be of good courage. Don't run from the attacks or the problems but face them in faith, confidence and courage. God says, "IF YOU WILL FACE IT, I WILL FIGHT IT".

Fear is the activity of servants but you are not servants; you are Royal sons and daughters of the King of kings. Be courageous! This is not a suggestion or a good idea. This is a command for all that will live in the way of Royalty. The enemy works to separate you from this courageous mindset. It is called DIS-couragement. The moment you are not willing to face challenges and oppositions with courage is the moment God can no longer use you.

Let us take a look at the life of Elijah to see this important point:

"When Ahab got home, he told Jezebel everything Elijah had done, including the way he killed the prophets of Baal. So Jezebel sent this message to Elijah: May the gods strike me and even kill me if by this time tomorrow I have not killed you just as you killed them. Elijah was AFRAID and FLED for his life . . . He sat down under a solitary broom tree and prayed that he might die. I have had enough, Lord, he said. Take my life, for I am no better than my ancestors who have already died . . . . And the voice of the Lord said, What are you doing here Elijah? He replied again, I have zealously served the LORD GOD Almighty . . . I am the only one left, and now they are trying to kill me, too. Then the LORD told him, Go back the same way you came . . . and anoint Elisha son Shaphat from the town Abel-meholah TO REPLACE YOU as my prophet." **1 Kings 19:1-4, 14-16**

Notice that Elijah is on the run, fleeing for his life in fear that the wicked Queen Jezebel would kill him. Elijah the royal representative of God who just stopped it from raining for 3 1/2 yrs, the one who was fed by ravens, the one who killed the prophets of Baal is now running in fear. He showed so much courage in times past but now after giving ear to the threats of Jezebel he is dis-couraged and fearful. That's how the enemy works, if he can get you to give ear to his words he can separate you from your courage and cause you to be discouraged and fearful.

Remember, the way of Royalty is to be courageous, so when God saw that Elijah was no longer courageous God REPLACED him (v.16). God has no room for weak, fearful, cowardly representatives. Our King is raising a mighty family of Royal Sons and Daughters who will stand courageously in faith and confidence in the face of the enemy. If you have been Dis-connected from your courage (discouraged) now is the time to Re-connect and believe the word of God with courageous faith. Royalty are those who are courageous!

CHAPTER 10

Royalty is Self-Less

and Never Self-Ish

Royalty is Selfless and Never Selfish…

Let me begin by informing you that the purpose for the position of authority is to administer help to the people. There is never a proper private or personal motive for authority. As representatives of the Kingdom of God we must understand that we have His wisdom, ability and might. We are not of this world but we are IN this world (see **John 17:14-15**). We do not live in this world as a vacation spot but we are planted in this world surrounded by the problems of the world to bring solutions to a world filled with problems.

"And as we live in God, our love grows more perfect. So we will not be afraid on the day of judgment, but we can face him with confidence because AS HE IS, SO ARE WE IN THIS WORLD." **1 John 4:17 (KJV)**

When Jesus was in the world he used his ability and wisdom to aid the hurting people. He would heal the sick and set at liberty those who were oppressed by the enemy. This is the purpose of the power or this is the assignment that comes with the authority. Notice in **Luke 4:18-19** the Holy Spirit comes to empower you to help others. This truth can be seen throughout the bible.

"So Jesus called them together and said You know that the rulers in this world and their authority) lord it over their people, and officers flaunt their authority over those under them. But among you it will be different. Whoever wants to be a leader (in a position of authority) must serve others. **Mark 10:42-43 (NLT)**

The Disciples were in pursuit of greatness but they were misguided by the desire of personal gratification. James and John were drawn by a desire to be great but their view of greatness is clouded by the world's conception of greatness. The world's view of authority and greatness is to be in a high position of power while others serve you. This polluted way of thinking has clouded the minds of the church and caused many to lose sight of the power that comes with serving others. Jesus brought a new way of thinking on the scene. He revealed greatness from the perspective of the Father. He said, "the rulers of this world flaunt their authority over those under them; But among you it will be different. Whoever wants to be a leader MUST serve (care for, aid, minister to, assist) others" (v.42-43). Jesus continues the lesson by using Himself as a blueprint for having power and authority and using it to help others.

"For even the Son of Man came not to be served but to serve others and to give his life as a ransom for many. **Mark 10:45**

As stated earlier there are many accounts that reveal this truth. Here is a lesson from the life of King Solomon.

"That night God appeared to Solomon and said, What do you want? Ask, and I will give it to you ! . . . Give me wisdom and knowledge to lead your people properly . . . God said to Solomon, Because your greatest desire is TO HELP YOUR PEOPLE, and you did not ask for wealth, riches, fame or even the death of your enemies or a long life, but rather you asked for wisdom and knowledge to properly govern my people. I will certainly give you the wisdom and knowledge you requested. But I will also give you wealth, riches, and fame such as no other king has had before you or will ever have in the future. **2 Chronicles 1:7-12**

The LORD greatly blesses Solomon with wealth and wisdom. Solomon had an open request from the Lord to receive anything he wanted and He chose wisdom for the purpose of properly leading the people. When God saw that Solomon was more concerned about helping the people than about receiving wealth, power or fame for himself God was then able to trust Solomon with all the things He didn't ask for, such as protection and peace because he displayed the way of royalty.

As ambassadors of the Kingdom of God we are never sent out powerless; but on the contrary, we are sent into a helpless, hopeless world filled with hurt, pain, disease, chaos and disaster and we are equipped with the power, wisdom and life of our King Jesus Christ to bring hope and change everywhere we go.

Prayer is closely related to this truth. As stated earlier. Jesus is a King that is focused on a Kingdom not a religion. **Isaiah 9:6** speaks of Jesus coming to the earth as a wonderful counselor, mighty father, everlasting God and prince of peace and he would come with a government on his shoulders. God has a body of believers to serve as governmental officials. We are to represent His government to a lost, dying world to reconcile sons back to the Father.

This is the very purpose of prayer. Prayer is not a religious act, there is nothing religious about it. Prayer is a governmental responsibility. It is when the government of God is doing business. Prayer is a legislative session where the government representatives meet with the government head to establish the interest or will of the government and to present the needs of the people. It is through prayer we gain knowledge of the will of God and it is through prayer where we present the NEEDS OF THE PEOPLE.

The Royal official is a praying believer who is engaged in helping those who are hurting, lost, bound and oppressed by the enemy.

The Royal governmental official (the believer) has access to all that the Kingdom is and all that the Kingdom has for the purpose of helping others progress and elevate and establishing the rule of God in the earth.

CHAPTER 11

Royalty is Always Mindful of their

Position of Authority

Royalty is always related and connected to power. This power is positional. It is the authority that comes with being in the elevated position. Royalty is the embodiment of the Kingdom. When royalty speaks, the kingdom has spoken. To attack royalty is to attack is to attack the Kingdom. This why when the Lord stopped Saul on the road of Damascus he said, Why are you persecuting me Saul? (**Acts 9:4**) because to attack the representatives of God is to attack God Himself.

This elevated position of authority is the strength and victory of all we face in life. The bible declares that Jesus has been given a elevated position that sits far above all principality, power, might, dominion and every name that is named (**Ephesians 1:19-21**). The church is secure in that revelation but we must become secure in the fact that Jesus shares that very same elevated position of authority with His body.

It is hard to imagine your head to be separated from your body and it continues to function properly. Your head and your body are in the same place. If your head is on the 3rd floor then your body is on the 3rd floor. We see Jesus in the elevated position exercising authority over every devil, disease, sickness and any other problem but we must see ourselves in that same position of authority. We are not sitting in a lower, lesser position. We are His body and we sit where our head sits. We are joint-heirs with Him (**Romans 8:17**).

For he raised us up with Christ and seated us with him (elevated above every circumstance and condition) in the heavenly realms because we are united with Christ." **Ephesians 2:6**

This elevated position of authority is the royal position of every believer. Royalty are to always be mindful of their position of authority. As royalty we are to think from our position of authority, we are to speak from our position of authority at all times. In fact the position of authority we have as sons of God should determine how we function in life and respond to opposition. This position is Not based on our feelings or natural ability. We do not have to feel like we have authority because we know we are in the elevated position of authority. This position is a position that is far above every devil and demon.

"Behold! I have given you authority and power to trample upon serpents and scorpions, and [physical and mental strength and ability] over all the power the enemy [possess]; and nothing shall in any way harm you." **Luke 10:19 (Amplified)**

Notice this scripture tells us that we have authority over all the power of the enemy. The word authority deals with a position but the word power deals with bility or strength. The message the Father is getting out to His sons is our position is greater than all of satan's ability. We never have to leave our seat to deal with the devil because our authority is greater than his ability. His ability can cause problems, produce sickness and wreck havoc but we can sit in our elevated position of authority and drive out devils, solve problems, heal the sick, raise the dead and bring peace everywhere we go.

Remember the principle of authority is authority always flows down, it never flows up. Authority is applied to those who are under the position.

What is man, that thou art mindful than him? And the son of man that thou visitest him? For thou host made him a little lower than the angels (Heb. Elohim—God Himself), and host crowned him with glory and honour. THOU MADE HIM TO HAVE DOMINION OVER THE WORKS OF THOU HAND; and has put ALL THINGS UNDER HIS FEET. **Psalm 8:4-6**

So the Word of God clearly tells us that we were made or created with the purpose of having dominion or ruling over all the earth. This scripture says, "All things are under our feet (or control)". Everything in the earth is under us as Sons of God. It is not that Moses, Paul or even David had what we don't have, we are filled with the superior Spirit of God. The difference is not in our abilities but our mentalities. When we think from this position and speak from this position every devil, sickness, disease and every other problem will obey our authority.

The key is to always be mindful of this position of authority. We cannot afford to allow any problem, lie, doctor's report or anything else cause us to lose sight of our elevated position of authority. When we come face to face with a problem we should say to that problem, I am bigger than you and greater is he that is in me, you are under my authority', and then issue a command to that problem. We must live from this position and not live towards it. We must think and speak FROM this position and not think and speak TOWARDS it. We are seated with Him in Heavenly places.

Some believers have misconception concerning this truth and they believe they will reign but only when they get to heaven. So they live in fear, bondage, and defeat on earth waiting to reign in heaven. This is the work of religion.

Religion look for a future escape from the problems we face on earth but the Kingdom of God doesn't look to escape the world or it's problems but to face the problems in bold confidence and reshape the world. The Kingdom representative is filled with the ability, counsel and wisdom of the Spirit of our King (the Holy Spirit) to confront the problems and bring change right here and right now. " . . . the free gift of righteousness [putting them into right standing with Himself] reign as kings IN LIFE through the one man Jesus Christ . . ." **Romans 5:17 (Amplified)**

Notice this scripture tells us through grace and righteousness we reign as kings IN LIFE. It doesn't say through grace and righteousness WE WILL REGIN but it say we reign NOW! WE ARE IN AUTHORITY NOW! WE ARE KINGS NOW!

SALVATION STARTS NOW! ETERNAL LIFE STARTS NOW! HEALING IS RIGHT NOW! VICTORY OVER THE FLESH IS RIGHT NOW! Don't put off the covenant blessings of God for when you get to heaven. Receive it NOW!

The enemy works hard through religion and vain philosophies to get you feel guilty for accessing your rights as a royal citizen of the Kingdom of Heaven. Some have forfeited their regal right to be prosperous and live in abundance. Some are afraid to access the power, wealth and health of the Kingdom in fear of being rejected and ridiculed by religion.

Royalty never seek the approval of others. As Royalty we are secure in ourselves and the words of our Father who is the King of all kings. This is why Jesus wrote in **John 5:41 (New Living Translation)**, "Your approval means nothing to me."

This is your covenant, your inheritance get it now. One other thing comes to mind in this discussion concerning Royalty is, all who Royalty are Royal with no apologies. So do not apologize for reigning over sickness, disease or devils. Don't apologize for accessing your covenant inheritance NOW! Don't apologize for being Royal.

You are elevated with Christ,

You are empowered by the Holy Spirit,

You are redeemed by the blood of Jesus,

You have the Word of God,

You have the nature of Christ,

You are filled with the wisdom of God,

    You are chosen to be the royal governmental official representing the Kingdom of God and establishing the rule of God in the earth. You are unstoppable! God himself is your source.

    There is a danger in not ruling. The recompense for not ruling is bondage and slavery. You cannot afford to not rule. You must rise to place where you will use the name of Jesus as a welded sword being empowered by the Holy Ghost and begin to conquer, lead, dominate, reign, instruct, govern, subdue, direct, control and believe. If you don't rule it, it will rule you!

RULE OR BE RULED,

RELEASE THE RULER IN YOU!

SECTION THREE:

THE TRUTH ABOUT YOUR REDEMPTION

"Understanding *How* and
Why you became what you are"

CHAPTER 12

The NOW Reality of the Word

The church has lost the consciousness of the NOW REALITY of God's Word. Many have taken their rights and privileges in God's Kingdom and put them off into the future.

By overlooking the NOW REALITY of the Word we improperly use the nature of faith and turn prayer into a begging dreadful ritual.

Many make dysfunctional statements when it comes to receiving our rightful inheritance in Christ due to this way of thinking. Statements like: "God will do it in His timing", "It must not be God's will", or "I'm not there yet!". To them it is never a NOW REALITY it is always, "I am going to be" pushing the NOW blessing into the future.

Jesus has made all things available NOW! His sacrifice and cleansing was a past tense action to make His Word and Work a NOW REALITY in your life.

The Word of God is always for NOW!

- In whom we HAVE our redemption" (**Eph. 1:7**).

- "but you ARE washed, but ye ARE sanctified, but you ARE justified in the name of the LORD" (**1 Cor. 6:11**).
- "By His strips you ARE /WERE healed" (**Isa. 53:5; 1 Pet. 2:24**).
- "Greater is He that IS IN us than He that is in the world" (**1 John 4:4**).
- "You ARE complete IN Him" (**Col. 2:10**)
- "For by one offering He HATH PERFECTED forever them that are sanctified" (**Hebrews 10:14**)
- " . . . we ARE more than conquers . . ." (**Rom. 8:36**)
- "Thanks be to God who HAS BLESSED us with all spiritual blessings in heavenly places" (**Eph. 1:3**)
- "I CAN do all things through Christ which strengthens me" (**Phil 4:13**)
- "we ARE heirs of God, and if heirs; then joint heirs with Christ" (**Rom. 8:14-15**)

Notice how Jesus has put these great promises into the NOW. We are more than conquers NOW! We are the glorious church without spot, wrinkle, blemish or any such thing NOW!

Search the scriptures for the NOW REALTIES. You are not the weak trying to get strong. You are not the sick trying to get healed. You are not the sinner trying to be righteous. No! You are the strong NOW! You are the Healed NOW! You are the Righteous NOW! LIVE in the NOW REALITY of the Word of GOD.

CHAPTER 13

A New Creation Reality

"Therefore if any man be in Christ he is a new creature: old things are passed away; behold, all things are become new," **2 Corinthians 5:17**

The Word of God clearly tells us that when we crown Jesus as our Lord we are at that moment a New Creature or New Creation.

Very few believers live in the light of this revelation. Paul prayed in **Ephesians 1:18**, " . . . the eyes of your understanding being enlightened; that you may know . . .". He desired the people to really see what has actually taken place in this New Creation. What is the new creation? What does this new creation consist of?

Colossians 3:1 (NLT), "Since you have been raised to new life WITH Christ, set your sights [fix your attention] on the REALITIES of heaven . . ."

This is an important point because it teaches us two things:

1. We are to identify WITH Christ
2. There are REALITIES in Heaven we are to fix our eyes on.

First of all we are to identify with Christ. Many believers are saved but continue to identify with Adam. They see themselves as weak and sinful. This mind-set has hindered the church long enough. Paul said in Romans 6:4, " . . . we are buried with him by baptism into death: that like AS CHRIST WAS RAISED UP FROM THE DEAD BY THE GLORY OF THE FATHER, EVEN SO [or by the same power in the same way] WE SHOULD WALK IN THE NEWNESS OF LIFE".

We were baptized into Christ. The word baptize means:—"to identify with". Being a new creature means we have been born again and the new creature I am is the very thing He is in substance, activity, mind, speech and nature.

What happened from the cross to the throne

When Christ died to the rule of satan, you died to the rule of satan. When Christ died to the curse, you died to the curse.

When Christ died to sin and sickness you died to sin and sickness. Scripture tells us that after Jesus died he went to the depths of hell. In hell he overthrew the ranks of satan, sin, and sickness and stripped them of their power.

When Christ defeated the enemy and stripped them of their power, they are defeated and powerless to you as well. When Christ was raised from the dead with complete authority, you were raised with Him with complete authority. When

Christ was justified in spirit and declared perfect before the father, you were justified in spirit and declared perfect before the Father.

All of this is a reality in heaven because in heaven you are completely identified with Christ in His death, burial and resurrection.

In heaven it is a reality that you are free from the rule of satan and sin. In heaven it is a reality that you are healed and free from the oppression of sickness and disease. In heaven it is a reality that the enemy is defeated and stripped of his power. In heaven it is a reality that you have the very nature and authority of Christ Jesus Himself. In heaven it is a reality that you are justified, complete and perfected forever before the Father (see **Hebrews 10:10,14**).

This is what Paul tells us to set our sights on. This new creation reality is the thing we are to focus on. We are to identify with Christ the risen Lord and not Adam the fallen man.

You are to look to and at Jesus, because when you see Him you will see the New Creation you are. **Romans 8:29**, "For God knew his people in advance, and he choose them to become like his son, so that his Son would be the firstborn among many brothers and sisters" **(NLT).**

This is simply an act of faith. This New Creation reality has nothing do with our effort to become like Christ. We are born into this likeness and identity. The righteousness of God which is by faith (**Romans 3:22**). We are to simply believe that the work of Christ is a finished work, a complete work!

We are to grasp this New Life by faith. I have become all that He is because of what He did. Many believers are struggling in areas because they have failed to believe this biblical truth. They identify with Adam. They believe and confess his weakness, his sinful nature, his curse and his sickness. They never reach the place where they identify with Christ. Our faith and confession are to be IN Christ. We are to believe and confess His strength, His righteous nature, His blessings and His health are now all our inheritance forever.

One of the biblical principles of the Kingdom of God is "The power of the Kingdom is release through the spoken word". It is important to declare out of your mouth in faith the truth of God's word.

This New Creation Reality is appropriated by faith and released through confession. It can never be released through the realm of the senses. We miss the mark of receiving when we try to figure out "how" with our natural minds. Do not wrestle with reason, simply believe that what God has said about you is true.

Do not look at the things of the earth, fix your attention on the realities of heaven and declare in faith that what is a reality in heaven is a reality in you.

Declare you are strong. Declare you walk in the wisdom of God. Declare you are healed. Declare you are free from addictions and the bondage of sin. Declare that you are justified in spirit and you stand perfected before the Father. When opposing situations do not line up with the reality of heaven, refuse to focus on those things, cast the thoughts down (according to **2 Corinthians 10:3-5**) and declare the realities of heaven.

Declare publicly, boldly and with resounding confidence because Jesus made it a reality!

CHAPTER 14

The Purpose, Presence and Power

of the Holy Ghost

Jesus declared to His disciples, "It is BEST for you that I go away, because if I don't, the Advocate [Holy Spirit] won't come . . ." **John 16:7 (NLT).**

Why was it more important for Jesus to leave? Jesus healed the sick, raised the dead, fed the hungry. Whenever the disciples had a problem Jesus would provide a answer. But now Jesus is leaving and he tells them that it is best for YOU that I go. The reason it would be better for them was so the Holy Ghost would come.

The Holy Ghost was the source of Jesus earthly ministry

Acts 10:38 reveals this truth, " . . . God anointed Jesus . . . with the Holy Ghost and with power: who went about doing good, and healing all that were oppressed of the devil . . .".

The power to heal the blind, raise the dead, cast out devils and bring solutions to very problem in Jesus' earthly ministry was produced by the Holy Ghost.

Luke 4:1, "And Jesus being full of the Holy Ghost returned from Jordan, and was led by the Spirit into the wilderness,"

Luke 4:14, "And Jesus returned in the power of the Spirit into Galilee: and there went out a fame of him through all the region round about."

Matthew 3:13-4:1, "Then cometh Jesus from Galilee to Jordan unto John, to be baptized of him. But John forbad him, saying, I have need to be baptized of thee, and comest thou to me? And Jesus answering said unto him, Suffer it to be so now: for thus it becometh us to fulfill all righteousness. Then he suffered him. And Jesus, when he was baptized, went up straightway out of the water: and, lo, the heavens were opened unto him, and he saw the Spirit of God descending like a dove, and lighting upon him: And lo a voice from heaven, saying, This is my beloved Son, in whom I am well pleased. Then was Jesus led up of the Spirit into the wilderness to be tempted of the devil."

Matthew 4:1, "Then was Jesus led up of the Spirit into the wilderness to be tempted of the devil."

Luke 4:18 (emphasis added), "The Spirit of the Lord is upon me because He [The Holy Ghost] has anointed (empowered) me to… {do the things God has assigned for me to do} . . ."

The same Holy Ghost is to be the source of your ministry as well

It was the Holy Spirit moving, working, speaking, and thinking through the first son. It is the desire of the Father to see the Holy Spirit move, work, speak and think through all sons.

Romans 8:11 tells us that we have the same Holy Ghost of the Lord Jesus Christ, "The Spirit of God, who raised Jesus from the dead, lives IN YOU. And just as God raised Christ Jesus from the dead, he will give life to your mortal bodies BY THE SAME SPIRIT LIVING WITHIN YOU" (NLT).

Many believers have functioned unconsciously to this truth. The mighty, miracle working Spirit that raised Christ from the dead is living WITHIN every believer.

If the believer is truly conscious of this he or she would not entertain the threats of the enemy. He would not faint when faced with trials of any kind. He would act in boldness overthrowing every form of affliction, oppression, addiction and habit by the Power of the Spirit of God.

The Father caused you to be filled WITH the SAME source of Jesus' earthly ministry and its success that you can have success at what He has called you to do as well. HE IS THE SAME HOLY GHOST!

THE (6) FOLDPURPOSE OF THE HOLY GHOST

The Holy Spirit comes to live in you with great purpose. That purpose is to empower you to be a witness (**Acts 1:8**), to be the greater in you and make you greater (**1 John 4:1-4**), to teach you all things (**1 John 2:20, 27**), to guide you into all truth (**John 16:13-15**), to make intercession for you according to the will of the Father (**Romans 8:26-28**), to reveal the mind of the Father to you (**1 Corinthians 2:9-13**). The Holy Ghost comes for the same reason as He came upon Christ as He was being baptized by John the Baptist in the Jordan river and that is to equip you to destroy the works of the devil.

You may be saying you are weak but the Holy Ghost has made you strong, wise, walking in power and authority to conquer and overthrow every devil, demon and sickness that comes your way.

Begin to agree with the Spirit of God living in you. You must expect the Holy Spirit to deal with you as He dealt with Jesus in His earthly ministry.

He makes you greater than any devil, sickness or disease. You are greater than any problem or circumstance. " . . . Greater is He that is in you than He that is the world . . ." (**1 John 4:4**).

Your confidence to face any problem in life should come from you consciousness of the presence, purpose and power of the Holy Ghost.

Chapter 15

Living "IN", "FOR" & "WITH" Christ

What does it mean to live FOR, IN and WITH Christ? We have majored in the subject of Living FOR Christ by living holy before the Lord and being witnesses sharing the gospel, pointing the lost to His salvation. We have also developed a heightened awareness of what it means to Live IN Christ accessing the redemptive right of justification and forgiveness. However the church has overlooked that we are to also live WITH Christ as well.

To live WITH Christ is to completely identify with Him. To live FOR Christ is occupational. To live IN Christ is positional, but to live WITH Christ is relational. When we live WITH Christ we identify with all He is and all He has.

When we arrive to this place we realize that He is not just our Lord but our elder brother and we are what he is in substance, nature, speech, mind and activity.

There are (3) Vital realities of living WITH Christ:

1. His authority becomes your authority.

Colossians 3:1 says, " . . . If you have been risen WITH Christ . . .". Notice the scripture says you have been risen WITH Christ and not risen BY Christ. To be risen BY Christ would imply that Jesus got up first and then He came and raised you up. Although this is chronologically correct it is not the mindset the Father wants us to take. He wants us to identify with Christ to the extent that when He rose you rose WITH Him.

He didn't just rise from the dead but He stripped the devil of all of His power and he rose, "with all authority . . . in heaven and in earth" (**Matthew 28:18**). This is the condition and position of which He rose into. If you were risen WITH Him you rose into the same authority. The authority over every problem is yours to use against every problem.

2. His relationship with the Father becomes your relationship with the Father.

Jesus said in His prayer for all believers, may they experience such perfect unity [that they may know] that you love them AS MUCH as you love me" (**John 17:23, NLT**). The person who lives WITH Christ understands this union with Father. The Father loves you in the exact same way that He loves Jesus. He doesn't have a lesser, lower love for you.

It is written in scripture that Jesus WAS the only begotten Son but He is no longer the only begotten. He is the, "first born of many brethren" (**Rom. 8:29**), because "you are no longer a servant but a son; and if a son then a heir of God through Christ" (**Gal. 4:7**).

His work of redemption was successful in bringing many sons unto Glory, (**Hebrews 2:10**) and "now Jesus and the ones He makes holy have the SAME Father. That is why Jesus is not ashamed to call them His brothers . . .", (**Hebrews 2:11, NLT**).

However the Father view Jesus is how He views you. However the Father deals with Jesus is how He deals with you. May you hear the words of the Father as the older brother of the prodigal son heard them as the Father speaks to you, "ALL that I have is yours" (**Luke 15:31**).

3. His inheritance becomes your inheritance.

Finally, living WITH Christ means you share all things with Him.

Romans 8:17 tells us that we are children of God and "heirs of God, joint heirs "WITH" Christ . . .".

To be a joint-heir is totally different than being a co-heir. A co-heir means you split everything down the middle but a joint-heir means you share everything equally.

You are a joint heir with Christ. His inheritance is your inheritance. If He receives anything from the Father He has to share it with you. You have legal access to all that Christ has and all that He is.

You do not have to work for it, you inherit it. "He that spared not His own Son, but delivered him up for us all, how shall he not WITH Him ALSO FREELY give us ALL Things" (Rom. 8:32). For we have received "the Spirit which is of God which is of God; that we might KNOW the things that are FREELY given unto us . . ." (**1 Cor. 2:12**).

We have spent much of our energy trying to obtain something that is freely given to us. We have fasted, prayed, cried and endured many religious rituals when all we need to do is understand His inheritance becomes our inheritance and it is freely given to us. "Always thanking the Father. He has enabled you to SHARE in the inheritance . . ." (**Col. 1: 12, NLT**).

The father is not desiring zealous servants but passionate sons. He is seeking they who are ready to not only live FOR or IN Christ but they who are living WITH Christ. You cannot effectively live FOR Christ if you do not see yourself IN Christ. However, the honor of living IN Him is wasted if you are not going to live WITH Him.

One example of living WITH Christ is in **Acts 3:1-9**. Peter is on his way to the temple for prayer and as they are entering the courtyard there is a man at the gate begging for money. Peter fixed His eyes on the man and said look at us and the man looked at them expecting to receive something from them and Peter told him, I don't have any silver or gold for you but I will give you what I have; In the name of Jesus Christ of Nazareth rise up and walk" (**Acts 3:6**).

Notice the manner in which Peter responded to the man's problem. He doesn't pray for permission, He acts with boldness extending the authority and name of Christ as if it is His name and authority. You too can respond with the same assurance. You have the power of attorney to use the authority of Christ to overturn any and every devilish situation. Living FOR Christ is your duty. Living IN Christ is your position but Living WITH Christ is your privilege.

Chapter 16

You Have What It Takes

Many believers are lost in the land of "have nots". You have been told that you are worthless, no good, weak sinners for so long until it has become attached to your consciousness. Your focus is on weakness because you have been told you do not have strength. Your focus is on sin because you have been told that you are a sinner by nature. The land of the have nots is a place where royal, strong, godly believers live as weak, sinful, sickly slaves because they are ignorant of what they actually have and are in Christ!

The word life (Gr. ZOE`) means divine nature. When the Jesus says in **John 17:2**, "As thou hast given him power over all flesh, that he should give eternal life to as many as thou hast given him". He is really saying He will give you His very own nature, the very nature of the Father. Don't get me wrong, heaven is a promise of blessed hope but Eternal life is the nature of the Eternal One in you even NOW as your very own nature.

We have this nature the moment we accept Jesus as Lord and we are filled with the Spirit of God to be recreated into the likeness of the first son Jesus Christ (Rom. 8:29).

John 5:11 says, " . . . God hath given to us eternal life (His very own nature)".

This is righteousness revealed. Righteousness has nothing to do with what you do, it is who you are. Holiness deals with your actions but righteousness is the nature of the Lord in you as your very own nature. This is the purpose of redemption. The blood of Jesus was shed for all of mankind to truly make you righteous (possessing the very nature of the Lord).

The nature of the Father is the ability, wisdom, life, character and attitude of the Father and it is in you!

The word of God is given to train you to live and display this new nature that is now in you. The bible says it this way, "All scripture is given by inspiration of God, and is profitable for doctrine, for reproof, for correction, for instruction in righteousness . . ." (**2 Tim. 3:16**).

2 Peter 1:3-4 (NLT), "By his divine power, God has given us everything we need for living a godly life . . . he has given us great and precious promises. These are the promises that ENABLE you to SHARE his divine nature".

We have this ability, life, wisdom and mindset in us now! The fruit of the Spirit are not things we have to pursue. They are the attributes we now have in our recreated spirits.

His nature is not optional! As His kids we must have His DNA or nature. This is not based on any work of your own (**Eph. 2:8-9**). This is a product of the finished, redemptive work of Christ. **Eph. 2:10** says, "You are His workmanship (or the product of His work)". In other words He made you righteous. You cannot make yourself righteous. You do not grow into righteousness. No, You are MADE righteous. The scripture says, "For he hath made him to be sin for us, who knew no sin; that we might be MADE the righteousness of God in him" (**2 Cor. 5:21**). You don't get to choose to be righteous after rebirth, you get to choose to display it. Receiving the nature of the Father is not optional!

The thought of you having the nature (ability, wisdom, or character) of the Father is the IDEA of the Father and the WORK of Christ. It is a GIFT (**Rom. 5:17**). We must learn to how think with this new mind we have. We must learn how to release this new ability we now possess. We must learn to display this new character we are. We must learn to give place to this new wisdom we now have.

This is the purpose of the Word of God. The word of God renews the mind of the believer that we may prove (or experience) this newness of life (**Rom. 12:2**). The word of God is the tool of the Holy Ghost. What a hammer is in the hand of a builder, so is the Word to the Holy Spirit. He brings us into the knowledge of this newness we have in Christ and our union with the Father through the Word of God.

John 5:12 says, "He that hath the Son hath life (the very nature of the Father)". Notice two things in this scripture:

1. The only requirement to receive nature is to believe on Christ.
2. You have this life or nature NOW!

You don't have to wait until you get to heaven to experience this life. If you have Christ YOU HAVE IT NOW!

1 John 5:13 also gives the purpose of the Word of God, "These things have I written unto you that believe on the name of the Son of God; that ye may KNOW that you HAVE eternal life (the very nature or life of the Eternal One)".

The word doesn't tell you what to become, it tells you what you are now that you have the nature of the Father. The word doesn't tell you what you need, it tells you what you now have because of your union with Christ.

All who are in Christ have the light of life (John 8:12). The word LIGHT in the Greek is foce` and it means the ability to manifest. All who are born of the Spirit have the ability to manifest the life of God. You have the ability to manifest this nature, ability, wisdom, character and mindset everywhere you go. You have become what He is, " . . . because as he is, so are we [not when we get to heaven but] in this world". (1 John 4:17).

You have the Holy Spirit and the Word of God. The wisdom of the Lord flows freely through you. You have the very nature of the Lord. Through Christ you have become unstoppable. YOU HAVE WHAT IT TAKES!

Chapter 17

The Truth About Righteousness

Christ and His Kingdom have been greatly misrepresented mainly due to the lack of confidence, boldness and faith of the church. The body of Christ has been commissioned to take on the same assignment of the great head of the church Jesus Christ. The assignment of Christ is expressed in **1 John 3:8**, "He that committeth sin is of the devil; for the devil sinneth from the beginning. For this purpose the Son of God was manifested, that he might destroy the works of the devil."

This assignment has been transferred from the head to the body of Christ. **John 14:12**, "Verily, verily, I say unto you, He that believeth on me, the works that I do shall he do also; and greater works than these shall he do; because I go unto my Father."

What has happened to the powerful, forceful body of believers that started in the upper room and later invaded the known world with the truth and power of the Kingdom of God?

The body of victorious believers has functioned with doubt and insecurities; tolerating the terrorizing attacks of the enemy because the body has shifted from true righteousness in Christ. Righteousness produces a boldness to act on every word from God.

SPIRITUAL BEINGS

The entirety of the Pauline Epistles was written to reveal the condition of the recreated, reborn believer. Many believers wrestle with the spiritual low self-esteem and mainly because they fail to see themselves as the spiritual beings they are. Majority of believers have identified themselves with their flesh but man is a spirit who functions in the earth through his flesh.

Hebrews 12:9, "Furthermore we have had fathers of our flesh which corrected us, and we gave them reverence: shall we not much rather be in subjection unto the Father of spirits, and live?"

The spirit was created to be just like the Father.

Genesis 1:26, "And God said, Let us make man in our image, after our likeness: and let them have dominion over the fish of the sea, and over the fowl of the air, and over the cattle, and over all the earth, and over every creeping thing that creepeth upon the earth."

Genesis 5:1 (NLT), "This is the written account of the descendants of Adam. When God created human beings, he made them to be like himself."

The true identity of man is he is a spirit housed in a body and he possesses a soul. The reborn believer is born or recreated a son of God. He doesn't have to work to become one. He is made a Son.

Galatians 4:6-7, "And because ye are sons, God hath sent forth the Spirit of his Son into your hearts, crying, Abba, Father. Wherefore thou art no more a servant, but a son; and if a son, then an heir of God through Christ."

John 1:12, "But as many as received him, to them gave the power to become the sons of God, even to them that believe on his name . . ."

He is a victor, a conqueror, a dominator created to live in unhindered union with the Father (see **John 17:21**).

The church has traded the identity of the spirit for the identity of the flesh. The church has preach condemnation and called it righteousness.

E.W. Kenyon writes in His book: TWO KINDS OF RIGHTEOUSNESS. "*Man has a highly developed sin-consciousness, a spirit inferiority complex, sense of unworthiness that dominates him. He is doubt ruled . . . The Sense of condemnation has given him an Inferiority Complex that makes him a coward. It robs him of faith in himself, in man, in God and in His word. This sin-consciousness holds him in bondage . . ."*

This condemnation came with the fall of man and did not exist prior to the fall. Allow the truth about righteousness to cause you to experience the redemptive work of Christ.

MAN IS A SPIRIT THEREFORE HE WILL NEVER BE SATISFIED WITH THE THINGS OF THE SENSES.

Begin your journey of understanding righteousness today!

Chapter 18

What is Righteousness?

The most desired thing of mankind is righteousness. Righteousness is defined as:

- *The ability to stand in the presence of God with no sense of sin, inferiority, guilt, condemnation or shame.*
- *To possess the perfect nature of the God as your very own nature.*

All forms of religions provide a plan or pathway that leads to emptiness be-cause they cannot remove the consciousness or damaging effects of sin. God approached and handled the sin problem in His Son Jesus Christ.

Romans 5:10, "For if, when we were enemies, we were reconciled to God by the death of his Son, much more, being reconciled, we shall be saved by his life."

He has forever dealt with sin in the sacrifice of His Son.

Hebrews 10:10, "By the which will we are sanctified through the offering of the body of Jesus Christ once for all."

The atonement of Christ, the redemptive work of our Lord makes man alive. A spiritually dead man cannot stand in God's presence.

The redemption of Christ was not an accident! It was a predetermined plan with a specific purpose (see **Ephesians 1:5,9,11**). The success of the redemption plan is based on it achieving the intended goal or purpose of the plan. What was the purpose or the goal? The goal of redemption was to cleanse man of sin making righteous that He can be filled with the Spirit of God. Jesus purposely went to the cross, purposely went to hell, paid the penalty of sin, purposely conquered satan, death and the grave to purposely make man righteous once again. It all was a part of the plan.

Jesus stated His purpose in **John 10:10**, "The thief cometh not, but for to steal, and to kill, and to destroy: I am come that they might have LIFE, and that they might have it more abundantly". The word LIFE comes from the Greek word `ZOE and it means nature or godly nature. The goal of Jesus was to make it so you can receive the very nature of God as your very own nature. Everything of your past is gone, you are new and the new creation you are is truly righteous.

2 Corinthians 5:17-18, "Therefore if any man be in Christ, he is a new creature: old things are passed away; behold, all things are become new. And all things are of God, who hath reconciled us to himself by Jesus Christ, and hath given to us the ministry of reconciliation."

A redemption that doesn't make you truly righteous is a failure. Religion has presented lies that has hindered us from experiencing this righteousness. Religion has presented limited righteousness that is obtained through works or good deeds. We have thought that if I pray enough, give enough or go to church enough I can be right with God.

Righteousness has nothing to do with what we DO. It is has everything to do with what He DID. Righteousness is a state of BEING, Holiness is a state of DOING. Dogs bark because it is in their nature to bark. The barking is the corresponding actions to its nature. Until we understand we have the perfect nature of the Father as our very own nature we will not have corresponding actions. Holiness is the result of Righteousness.

We have been told that we are sinners and no one can live above sin. This is completely contradicting towards the word of God.

Ephesians 4:24, "And that ye put on the new man, which after God is created in righteousness and true holiness.

Colossians 1:22 (NLT), "Yet now he has reconciled you to himself through the death of Christ in his physical body. As a result, he has brought you into his own presence, and you are holy and blameless as you stand before him without a single fault

Colossians 2:10, "And ye are complete (perfect, without flaws, finished) in him, which is the head of all principality and power:"

Hebrews 10:14, "For by one offering he hath perfected for ever them that are sanctified".

Romans 6:22, "But now being made free from sin, and become servants to God, ye have your fruit unto holiness, and the end everlasting life".

Jude 1:24, "Now unto him that is able to keep you from falling, and to present you fault-less before the presence of his glory with exceeding joy,"

We must come to the place where we trust the word of God over the traditions of men, denominational doctrines and religious ideologies. We do not have to wait until we get to heaven be righteous.

The Father declares all who trust in Christ is justified or not guilty and gives you his very own nature. The nature of God is my nature. The Father says, I am love; I too say, I am love. Do not wait to go to heaven to believe. Jesus put away sin, died as our substitute and rose from the dead as the first fruit from the dead. When we crowned Him as the Lord as the Lord of our lives at that moment we receive God's nature and become righteous.

2 Corinthians 5:21, "For he hath made him to be sin for us, who knew no sin; that we might be made the righteousness of God in him."

Again, do not wait to go to heaven to walk in this righteousness. You are Righteous NOW! You have God's nature NOW! You are more than conquerors NOW! You belong in God's presence. You are new and mighty. You are reborn, revived and repositioned. You can stand in God's presence with Boldness. Be the Righteousness of God in Christ Jesus!

Chapter 19

The Damaging Effects of Sin-Consciousness and the Restoring Work of Righteousness

Again, the true identity of man is spiritual. He is a spirit who lives in a natural body. When Adam fell in sin it affected and infected all of mankind. He fell from the spirit to the natural. Because disobedience to the instruction of the Lord and because of that he immediately died (not physically but spiritually). The word *die* in **Genesis 2:17** means - *to wither, to be separated from the life source*. Adam died physically because he was dead spiritually.

However, we can immediately see the effects of sin-consciousness at work in Adam. In **Genesis 3:7-10** we see Adam attempting to repair a spiritual problem with natural means. He becomes afraid and finds a hiding place to hide from the presence of God. Then in v. 10 we see Adam filled with guilt and shame. These are the effects of sin consciousness. It produces shame, fear and cause one to try to repair their relationship with God with natural means. This is a sin disease!

Genesis 3:7-10, "At that moment their eyes were opened, and they suddenly felt shame at their nakedness. So they sewed fig leaves together to cover themselves. When the cool evening breezes were blowing, the man and his wife heard the LORD God walking about in the garden. So they hid from the LORD God among the trees. Then the LORD God called to the man, "Where are you?" He replied, "I heard you walking in the garden, so I hid. I was afraid because I was naked."

E.W. Kenyon writes in Two Kinds of Righteousness, "*Man has sought to heal this awful disease called sin. The sense of unworthiness destroys faith, robs us of our peace of mind, make ineffectual the most earnest and zealous prayer life. It robs us of all fellowship and communion with the Father.[Man has tried to cure it Himself]. Man's cure has been repentance of sins, sorrow for sins and deep agony in prayer. Others have tried to quiet their consciences by going to church, doing penance, fasting, giving money, saying prayers, doing good deeds, giving up pleasures, confessing their sins, fighting bad habits, putting themselves under discipline of self-denial and self-abasement, neglecting the body. Some have even gone so far as to lacerate their bodies. Others have even taken long pilgrimages*".

All of those methods have been tried but none have been successful to get rid of the consciousness of sin. Mainly, because they are natural attempts to repair a spiritual problem. Much of the damage concerning sin consciousness has taken place at the church through religion of some kind.

Pastors and Laymen of all sort have flooded the pulpit to preach sin. The preaching of sin never cures the sin problem. The preaching of sin strengthens condemnation. The solution is righteousness through Christ. Preaching of sin not only condemns but it makes even the most anointed preacher feel weak and inferior. The awful attitude of unworthiness that we call humility that circulates through the church is a result of sin consciousness.

Religion has preached that worship is an experience where I have to work to get into God's presence. They have said things like, we must press into His presence. Press into what? Press through what? The veil has been torn down, we have unhindered access and the scripture tells us these things in **Hebrews 4:14-16 (Message Translation)**, "Now that we know what we have Jesus, this great High Priest with ready access to God let's not let it slip through our fingers. We don't have a priest who is out of touch with our reality. He's been through weakness and testing, experienced it all, all but the sin. So let's walk right up to him and get what he is so ready to give. Take the mercy, accept the help".

The goal of the Father was not to blanket our sins. In the old testament acts of atonement the blood of bulls and goats covered the sins of the people. New testament redemption is the blood of Christ cleansing the sins of the people. The old covenant deals with hiding or covering your sins but the new covenant deals with the removing of your sins. This removing and cleansing of sin deals with the removing of the sin nature giving you the very nature of God, removing the acts and the effects empowering you in the acts of righteousness, and removing the consciousness of sin and renewing your mind to be conscious of righteousness.

The whole goal of Christ's redemption was to totally cleanse sin including the conscience of it as well. Hebrews 9:9, "Which was a figure for the time then present, in which were offered both gifts and sacrifices, that could not make him that did the service perfect, as pertaining to the conscience;"

Hebrews 10:1-2, "For the law having a shadow of good things to come, and not the very image of the things, can never with those sacrifices which they offered year by year continually make the comers thereunto perfect. 2For then would they not have ceased to be offered? because that the worshippers once purged should have had no more conscience of sins."

The Holy Spirit is at work to unveil to you the truth about righteousness and cause you to become conscious of it. Very few believers have faith in their state of righteousness in Christ. They have faith in the inability of the flesh or the sinful state of the unsaved, fallen man. They lack faith in the fact that they are a new creature, born again, possessing the very nature of God as their very own nature.

There are only two reasons for the a person possessing a sin conscious mindset.

1. THE PERSON HAS NEVER TRUSTED JESUS AS THE LORD AND BENN BORN AGAIN.
2. THE PERSON HAS NEVER GROWN BEYOND THE STATE OF BABY-HOOD AND DOESN'T KNOW THEIR RIGHTS, STANDING AND PRIVI-LEGES IN CHRIST.

This is the fruit of the redemptive work of Christ, we have lost the sense of sin and in its place we receive the sense of oneness and fellowship with the Father that Christ Himself experiences, even now do we experience this.

Our standing is restored, our fellowship is restored, our faith is restored, our peace is restored, our relationship is restored and Sonship is given. We are not servants! We are not sinners! We are sons who have the very nature of the Father and we stand in His presence with NO sense of guilt, fear, shame or inferiority of any kind. We are righteous!

Chapter 20

The Source of Righteousness

Our standing with the Father is solely upon the work of Christ Jesus and our faith in Christ makes us righteous. It is because of Jesus we are saved, justified and made righteous. It sounds simple doesn't it? It is simple on our end but religion has complicated it with their teachings and attempts to be made right with the Father through what they do.

Again I say that this great redemption is one that is filled with purpose. What was the purpose of the Father? What was He believing to get out of offering His only Son to die?

The Father's goal was perfection in man! His goal was righteousness. Anything less than righteousness, anything less than perfection is a failure.

I know you have heard all of your life that we are, no good sinners and nobody is perfect. This kind of thinking is the fruit of sense knowledge. It is the wisdom of the earth realm. Let us search the scriptures to find out what the Father says on the subject.

Matthew 5:48, "Be ye therefore perfect, even as your Father which is in heaven is perfect."

We are instructed to be perfect. These are the words of Christ. The Father reveals the purpose of the Redemption of Christ clearly in **Hebrews 7:11, (NLT)** "So if the priesthood of Levi, on which the law was based, could have achieved the perfection God intended, why did God need to establish a different priest-hood, with a priest in the order of Melchizedek instead of the order of Levi and Aaron?".

The old order of atonement was inadequate because it could not produce the perfection the Father intended. **Hebrews 7:19 (NLT)** clearly defines this point. "For the law never made anything perfect. But now we have confidence in a better hope, through which we draw near to God".

Jesus became our sin Substitute, taking our place and becoming a sin offering for all of mankind. When Jesus rose from the dead and was declared righteous all who believe in Him was declared righteous thus becoming perfect at that moment.

Romans 4:25 says Jesus was justified or made righteous. **1 Timothy 3:16** says Jesus was, "justified in the spirit". 1 Peter 3:18 says that He was, "made alive in spirit". Hebrews 10:10 says we are sanctified by the offering of Christ and Hebrews 10:14 says those who are sanctified are forever made perfect through the redemptive work of Christ.

The word **PERFECT** is defined as:

- *to be finished, sound, whole and complete, without flaws.*

Colossians 2:10 says we are made COMPLETE or *perfect* in Him who is the head of all principality and power.

For years we have wrestled with the unrighteous mindset of being incomplete and unworthy but **2 Corinthians 5:17-18** expresses the proper mindset towards our redemption. Where it reads, "Therefore if any man be in Christ, he is a new creature: old things are passed away; behold, all things are become new. And all things are of God, who hath reconciled us to himself by Jesus Christ, and hath given to us the ministry of reconciliation; ".

We are new creatures, new creations. Whatever is old is gone! All of the old is gone, not just portions of it but all of it! Verse18 said that everything in this new creature that I am IS OF GOD. In other words there is nothing in the new me that is not like God. I have the nature of the Father as my own nature.

Listen to the talk of the sense knowledge of the religion. "Nobody is perfect, we are all sinners saved by grace". This is fallacy at its greatest. We cannot be the sinner and the saved. We are correct if we say, we were the sinners but we have been saved by grace. You cannot have the nature of sin and satan and have the nature of the Lord. This would mean as a believer you would have two Fathers.

The word perfect in the New Testament has a few different meanings.

The majority comes from two Greek words which are:

- Tel-i-oo: *to be accomplished, complete, finished and without flaws.*
- Tel-i-os: *to grow into the knowledge or to mature in character.*

Every scripture that mentions the word PERFECT cannot be properly translated as maturity as some suggest. **Hebrews 10:14**, " . . . he has perfect forever", is the Greek word tel-i-oo: to be without flaws. He has made us new and now we are perfect, cleansed, righteous without flaws. **Colossians 1:22 (NLT)** says we, " . . . stand before Him without a single fault". **Ephesians 4:13** says the ministry gifts of Pastors, Evangelist, Apostles, Prophets and Teachers are to raise the body of Christ up until we come into the unity of the faith, "unto a perfect man' is the Greek word tel-i-os: to grow and mature in knowledge.

A powerful example of the usage of these two words at work in scripture is **Philippians 3:12-15**, "12. Not as though I had already attained, either were already *perfect*: but I follow after, if that I may apprehend that for which also I am apprehended of Christ Jesus. 13. Brethren, I count not myself to have apprehended: but this one thing I do, forgetting those things which are behind, and reaching forth unto those things which are before, 14. I press toward the mark for the prize of the high calling of God in Christ Jesus. 15. Let us therefore, as many as be *perfect*, be thus minded: and if in anything ye be otherwise minded, God shall reveal even this unto you."

In v. 12 Paul says _He is not perfect_ and in v. 15 Paul says _He is perfect_. In v. 12 where Paul says He is not perfect he uses the Greek word tel-i-os and in v. 15 where he says he is perfect he used the Greek word tel-i-oo. Paul was speaking of the recreative, redemptive change he has experienced. He was saying in v.12 that I have not made it to the point where I aware of all that I have become because of Christ and in v.15 he was saying, but as many of us that are complete or perfect in Christ let us think like this. He was saying that every day we should grow into the knowledge of what Jesus has done in making us righteous.

Notice the bible tells us to grow in a lot of things, (i.e. grace, knowledge, faith, etc.) but we are never instructed to grow in righteousness. This is because when we place our faith in the risen savior and receive His Spirit we are made anew and this new creation is finished product. We are righteous now! Every day we grow in knowledge of what we are in Christ but we are ALL that we are in Christ Now!

This was the goal of the Father; to bring forth a perfect, complete, redeemed righteous man by nature and He did this through His Son Jesus Christ.

Let me list the perfections of Christ:

1. Jesus was a PERFECT sacrifice.
2. Jesus blood did a PERFECT cleansing

3. Jesus is a PERFECT High Priest

4. Jesus provided a PERFECT redemption

5. Jesus gave man His PERFECT nature

6. To produce a PERFECT man at New Birth.

It is not possible to have a PERFECT sacrifice, PERFECT cleansing, PERFECT High Priest, PERFECT redemption, PERFECT nature and still produce a IMPERFECT person.

You are not the sinner, worthless and filled with guilt. You are the Righteous forever perfected without flaws. Grow into the knowledge of all Christ has made you. He is the source of your perfection. You are righteous because of what He did.

James 5:16 says the prayers of the righteous is powerful in it's working. You are the righteous. Do not go into the Father's presence weakly, begging with your head down; that dishonors His plan, Son, Blood and Love. Go in prayer with confidence. Go into His presence with boldness because you have His nature as your very own nature. You have now become all that He is. You have His DNA. You are sound, whole and complete. You stand in his presence without any inferiority, guilt or shame because you are righteous. Let this confidence and boldness and standing with God drive out all acts of the flesh. Let it drive out all sickness and disease. Let it drive out all fear and lack. Let it cause you to see yourself the way God sees you which is strong, victorious, healed, delivered, wealthy, full of wisdom and light possessing His very nature!

Chapter 21

The Same Type of Son

It was never the Father's will to have servants. He never wanted church folks or religious followers but He wanted royal leaders who would bring Him glory in the earth living, walking, thinking, and speaking with His nature in them. He never wanted servants but he wanted sons who would serve.

John 1:12, "But as many as received him, to them gave he power to become the sons of God, even to them that believe on his name:"

When you crown Jesus as the Lord of your life something amazing happens. You go from being a weakling to being mighty. You go from being sickly to accessing the very health of God. You go from being a sinner to being the very righteousness of God. You go from being a servant to being a son. **Galatians 4:7** says, "Wherefore thou art no more a servant, but a son; and if a son, then an heir of God through Christ". All of heaven is at work to get you function in the Sonship you have received. THE HOLY SPIRIT HAS THE RESPONSIBILITY OF LEADING, TEACHING, TRAINING AND EMPOWERING ALL BELIEVERS TO FUNCTION AS SONS OF GOD.

As stated earlier, all of heaven is working to get you to function as a son but all of religion is working against the plan of the Father by working to make you a servant.

Romans 8:19, "For the earnest expectation of the creature waiteth for the manifestation of the sons of God".

All of creation is waiting on the real you to show up. The real you defeats darkness by using the word of God and the name of Jesus as a proven, sturdy welded sword. The real Notice the scripture points out the purpose of the redemptive work of Christ was to bring many sons into glory. It honors the Father for you to take advantage of such a great salvation to be the Son you were created to be.

A redemption that doesn't produce strong, righteous sons possessing the very nature, life and character of the Father is a failure.

This was the only thing the Father was focused on when He sent His only begotten son (**John 3:16**) because through this one seed, Jesus would become the first born among many brethren (**Rom. 8:29**).

Jesus goes from being the ONLY BEGOTTEN to being the FIRST BORN. The term FIRST BORN would imply that there will be others like Him born after Him

Again referring to Hebrews 2:11 it says, " . . . For both he that sanctifieth and they who are sanctified are all of one . . .". This is awesome! The scriptures tell us that Jesus (the sanctifier) and all believers (the sanctified) are ALL one or of the SAME substance.

This scripture is unveiling the truth that Jesus was not a different type of son than what we are. WE ARE THE SAME TYPE OF SON AS THE FIRST SON OUR LORD JESUS CHRIST! Whatever type of Son Jesus is that is the same type of son we are. The Father doesn't have a type "A" son and a type "B" son. Neither does He have step sons. It pleased the father to bruise Jesus or to send Jesus to die for mankind (**Isa. 53:10**). The death of Jesus was not a sad event but the Father willingly and gladly offered His ONLY son that He may receive MANY sons unto glory.

Now that we know we are the SAME type of son we should now expect the Father to deal with us as He dealt with Jesus the first son in His earthly ministry. THE FIRST SON IS THE PATTERN OR BLUEPRINT FOR ALL SONS.

We are the SAME type because the Father made sure that we have the SAME things.

- <u>We have the SAME Spirit</u>

Romans 8:11, "The Spirit of God, who raised Jesus from the dead, lives in you. And just as God raised Christ Jesus from the dead, he will give life to your mortal bodies by this same Spirit living within you".

You have the ability to manifest life and you are filled with the very wisdom of God. The real you is not a servant. No! You're a son of the Most High God.

Hebrews 2:10-12, "10 For it became him, for whom are all things, and by whom are all things, in bringing many sons unto glory, to make the captain of their salvation perfect through sufferings. 11For both he that sanctifieth and they who are sanctified are all of one: for which cause he is not ashamed to call them brethren,12Saying, I will declare thy name unto my brethren, in the midst of the church will I sing praise unto thee."

- We have the SAME inheritance

Rom. 8:16-17, "16The Spirit itself beareth witness with our spirit, that we are the children of God: 17And if children, then heirs; heirs of God, and *joint-heirs with Christ;* if so be that we suffer with him, that we may be also glorified together."

- We have the SAME assignment

1 John 3:8; John 14:12, " 8He that committeth sin is of the devil; for the devil sinneth from the beginning. For this purpose the Son of God was manifested, that he might destroy the works of the devil. 12Verily, verily, I say unto you, He that believeth on me, the works that I do shall he do also; and greater works than these shall he do; because I go unto my Father."

- We have the SAME unity with the Father

John 17:21, "21That they all may be one; as thou, Father, art in me, and I in thee, that they also may be one in us: that the world may believe that thou hast sent me."

- We have the SAME glory

John 17:22, "22And the glory which thou gavest me I have given them; that they may be one, even as we are one:"

- We have the SAME relationship with the Father

John 17:23, "23I in them, and thou in me, that they may be made perfect in one; and that the world may know that thou hast sent me, and hast loved them, as thou hast loved me."

- We have the SAME seat of authority

Eph. 1:20-22; Eph. 2:6, " 20Which he wrought in Christ, when he raised him from the dead, and set him at his own right hand in the heavenly places, 21Far above all principality, and power, and might, and dominion, and every name that is named, not only in this world, but also in that which is to come:22And hath put all things under his feet, and gave him to be the head over all things to the church 6And hath raised us up together, and made us sit together in heavenly places in Christ Jesus:

- We have the SAME mind

Phil. 2:5; 1 Cor. 2:16, "5Let this mind be in you, which was also in Christ Jesus: 16For who hath known the mind of the Lord, that he may instruct him? but we have the mind of Christ."

We must rise to the place where we understand that the SAME life that is in the seed is also in the fruit.

Now that Jesus has made sure that we have the SAME... we should live, function and dominate over darkness in the SAME way Jesus did in His earthly ministry. YOU ARE THE SAME TYPE OF SON!

Chapter 22

The Faith of the Father

Our God is a faith God. His Kingdom is a faith Kingdom. In fact faith is the currency of the Kingdom of God. What money is in our government is what faith is in God's government, you can get nothing done without it. "For without FAITH it is IMPOSSIBLE to please Him . . ." **Heb. 11:6**. This means we are recreated to be faith beings as well. We were not created to let our senses govern us but we were created to rise above the limitations of the natural by believing the truth of God's Word.

What is faith in relation to the believer? An effective definition for faith (*as it relate to the believer)* is:

- <u>FAITH</u>: *to be conscious of one's covenant, ability, identity and relationship with Christ with no respect to the senses.*

Our covenant tells us what we have, our ability tells us what we can do, our identity tells us what and who we are and our relation tells us who we are connected to.

This is the purpose of the Word of God, to build faith. Reading about the faith of others will not build faith in you, only the Word of God can build faith. "Faith cometh by hearing . . . and hearing . . . the Word of God" Rom. 10:17. The Word reveals the realities of these things and build within the believer a consciousness of them in your spirit until faith starts to rise.

Unbelief on the other hand in relations to the believer is:

- UNBELIEF: *the result of not having or losing consciousness of one's covenant, ability, identity and relationship with Christ by giving esteem to the senses.*

As long as you are focused on the eternal Word of God you will reign with Christ but the moment you esteem what is revealed to the senses you will begin to lose consciousness of all that you are and all that you have in Christ and faith will leave and doubt will rise. For, "we look not at the things which are seen (revealed to the senses) but the things that are unseen (the eternal Word of God) 2 Cor. 4:18.

THE FAITH OF THE FATHER

The Father has faith in (4) major areas:

1. He has faith in the finished work of Christ:

" . . . We are sanctified THROUGH THE OFFERING OF THE BODY of Jesus Christ ONCE AND FOR ALL . . . For by one offering He hath PERFECTED FOR-EVER them that are sanctified." **Heb. 10:10,14**

The Father has faith that the finished work of Christ (death, burial, and resurrection) would be enough to redeem you. He believed that it would be enough to break the hold of sin over your life. He believed that through that work you would be redeemed from all sickness and disease. He believed it would be enough to recreated you and make you truly righteous through that same work. He believed that what Jesus did would be enough to make you perfect and give you the very nature of the Father. He had faith in the finished work of Christ!

2. He has faith in the purpose, presence and power of the Holy Spirit.

"Little children, you are of God [you belong to Him] and have [already] defeated and overcome them [the agents of the antichrist], because He Who lives in you is greater (mightier) than he who is in the world". **1 John 4:4 (Amplified).**

That word Greater in this scripture actually means to be in overflowing abundance in quantity and ability. The Father believed that the Spirit of God would be more than enough to go through life victoriously. He believed that the Holy Spirit would be more than enough for you to live above sin, walk in authority and power, heal the sick, cast out devils and live like the Son of God you are. He believed the Holy Spirit would teach you the ways of the Kingdom, reveal the word of the King, empower you to do the work of the representative and guide you into all truth. He had faith in the Holy Ghost!

3. He has faith in the ability of the Word of God.

" . . . when ye received the word of God which ye heard of us, ye received it not as the word of men, but as it is in truth, the word of God, which effectually worketh also in you that believe." **1Thessalonians 2:13**.

Notice the scripture says the word effectually works in you. This reveals the ability of the Word of God. It is not just black words on white pages in a old book. No! It is alive! It is full of life. Every word from God has within it the ability to fulfill itself. There are no barren scriptures in the bible. Every scripture is pregnant and ready to give birth in your life. The Father had faith the Word would change your mindset and build faith. He had believed the Word would be enough to change your health, marriage, finances, or whatever you need. He believe the word would be enough to bring change in every area of your life. He believed in the Word of God!

4. He has faith in the believer.

"These miraculous signs will accompany those who believe: They will cast out demons in my name, and they will speak in new languages. They will be able to handle snakes with safety, and if they drink anything poisonous, it won't hurt them. They will be able to place their hands on the sick, and they will be healed." **Mark 16:17-18 (NLT).**

The Father is expressing His faith in the believer in the scripture. Notice He said THEY WILL cast out demons, THEY WILL speak in new languages, THEY WILL be able… , THEY WILL lay hands on the sick but all of this comes after the FAITH that THEY WILL BELIEVE! The Father believed that you would believe His word. He believed that you would embrace it, become one with it and apply it with action faith. He believed that you would seize the opportunity to do what the Word says. He believed that you would be the agent He used to combat the enemy and He believed that you would do it with courage. He believed in you!

THE FAITH OF ALL BELIEVERS

All believers should follow the Father's example and have faith in the same things. The Father had faith THAT THE FINISHED WORK OF Christ would make you righteous, perfect, possessing the very nature of the Father, so we should have faith the finished work of Christ HAS MADE us righteous, perfect, possessing the very nature of the Father.

The Father believed that the Spirit of God would be more than enough to handle any and every situation, so we should believe that the Spirit of God IN US is more than enough to handle any and every situation. The Father believed that the Word of God would change your mindset and change every situation in your life, then we should use the Word of God to change our mindset and change every situation in our life. The Father believed that the believer would operate in the same force and life as Jesus did in His earthly ministry, so we should operate with the same force and life in our earthly ministry.

THE FATHER HAS FAITH IN YOU, NOW IT IS TIME FOR YOU HAVE FAITH IN WHAT GOD HAS DONE IN YOU, THROUGH YOU AND TO YOU.

The content of this book speaks in reference to the reborn spirit-man. If you have not decided to make the Lord Jesus the Lord of your life and be filled with His Spirit now is the time. Open your heart and say the prayer below:

<u>Prayer</u>

Lord Jesus, I open my heart to you. I acknowledge

that you died and rose from the dead to bring me from

bondage to freedom and now I openly confess

that you are my LORD. I renounce the things of the

kingdom of darkness and I submit to your Lordship. Fill me with your Holy Spirit, teach me

through your Spirit that I may properly represent

you in the earth. I receive this by faith. In Jesus name, Amen!

If you prayed the prayer above, congratulations, welcome to the Kingdom of God. First thing you need to do is get a bible and read it, it is the constitution of this Kingdom: It reveals your purpose, rights and position in relation to this Kingdom. Secondly spend time in prayer and allow the Holy Spirit to teach you. Thirdly, find a bible teaching church home to grow with other believers. All of heaven is rejoicing for you right now! Confession I am spirit and not flesh, therefore today, I shall dominate, be victorious and increase in every area. My family shall be protected, my children shall be saved, my marriage shall prosper and my finances shall increase. Today, I shall walk in true identity, my spirit and not my flesh. I shall control my tongue and my mind regardless of how I feel, The word of God coming out of my mouth is just as powerful the word of God coming out of His mouth. And the joy of the Lord is my strength, And I refuse to let anybody or anything pull me down This day, In Jesus name, Amen!

More books to from Sozo Resources:

- Living According to the Standard by Dr. Johnny Young Jr
- Hope for the Minister by Dr. Johnny Young Jr
- The Breath of God -Daily Devotional by Dr. Johnny Young Jr
- The Innovation of Change by Kelsei LuBom
- Living From an Eternal Standpoint by Dr. Perry Petite
- Dating 101: Back to Basics: A Guide for Women by Dr. Troy N. Watson

Be sure to visit our school website: **www.hopebible.us**

For more info or to schedule for a speaking engagement contact

Dr. Johnny Young, Jr.

5700 Florida Blvd Suite 706

Baton Rouge, La 70806

Email: johnnyby1217@gmail.com

Office: (225) 439-4776

About the Author

Dr. Johnny Young, Jr. has served the body of Christ as a minister of the gospel for two decades of dedicated service. He has received a Bachelor Degree in Theology, a Master Degree in Communication and a Doctorate Degree in Theology. He has also received a Doctorate Degree in Psychology.

Dr. Young is the Founder and President of The H.O.P.E Bible Institute (which is nationally recognized, accredited and approved. With (5) Campuses this institution has developed into a leading organization to strengthen and develop Kingdom Ambassadors for the work of Kingdom Expansion.

Dr. Young is the author of the Nationally Released book, THE TRUTH ABOUT YOU, The Breath of god and many more. He is the overseer of Heavenly H.O.P.E Ministries. He is the President of J. Young, International as well as a chaplain for the state of Louisiana Department of Corrections. Although he is an entrepreneur, pastor, educator, author, father and husband, he prefers to be called a Son of God living service to man.